gather

gather

Fresh, tasty recipes for sharing

TIM READ

MasterChef New Zealand Winner

ALLEN&UNWIN

SYDNEY·MELBOURNE·AUCKLAND·LONDON

contents

introduction
6

pork
14

beef
34

chicken
52

game
76

lamb
88

seafood
102

desserts & sweets
124

the basics
148

acknowledgements
185

index
187

introduction

Food for me has always been about two things: gathering together the freshest of ingredients, and gathering together people to share in the event that is eating. This book, *Gather*, is a direct reflection of my food philosophy.

In my eyes, the kitchen is not the start of the process, nor is the dinner table the end of it. I believe food begins with the planting of a seed or the 5am start to a day fishing or hunting. From that point on, everything is part of the process towards the meal that ends up on the dining table – and it doesn't stop there, either. In a way, food continues beyond the moment in which it's eaten, through the friendships, memories and moments that are built and gathered during the entire process – things that last much longer than the final dish being washed and put away.

I have purposely tried to create recipes made for sharing at the table, with servings generous enough to feed any latecomers who turn up just as you're about to sit down. My hope is that you'll take the time to engage in the field-to-table process as early on as possible, and that you won't worry about rushing things. I hope you find the chance to enjoy first the time it takes to create a meal and then the pleasure that comes from sharing it with others.

Some people are born with a whisk in one hand and an oven mitt in the other; I'm not one of those people. Growing up, I was always far more interested in the outdoors, whether kicking a ball around the backyard or making up adventures with friends. Cooking for me was limited to a barbecue or what we called a 'hobo stove' – a small fire built under an upside-down 1-litre can, which we'd cook bacon and eggs on the top of.

When I went to university, a group of us boys began to do more and more spearfishing together, usually based at my friend Sam Milne's family beach house in Tawharanui. Scottie, Sam's dad, was

my first food hero and is the one responsible for turning my love of the outdoors into a love for the kitchen. At the Milnes' house, fish is a breakfast meal, so we would come back in the afternoon and prepare the fish for the next day's breakfast before moving on to dinner prep. Scottie is brilliant at including others, so we would all be involved in getting a dinner together that was usually based on a large cut of protein, cooked on the barbecue, with myriad vegetable accompaniments. I loved these times – all of us working together and sharing in the spoils of a hard day's work with an incredible dinner and a glass of wine, then again in the morning with fresh fish on toast.

The 'spark', however, was really ignited when I shot my first deer. With my crude understanding of animal anatomy, I decided to butcher it myself, cutting off the major steaks and reserving all the trimmings for salami. Then a group of uni mates and I congregated at the Milnes' house and hosted a dinner party, splashing out on some nice wine and serving a venison osso buco. The field-to-table process – starting with the hunt right through to being able to share food and create an occasion with friends – became one of my greatest joys.

As I began to collect more and more fresh produce, I also began to cook more and more – pigs, paua, crayfish, rabbit, duck and even mussels off the 200-metre buoy. When I put my mind to something I tend to go all out, and I guess that trait helped me to pretty rapidly improve my culinary skills. Cooking became a way of releasing my inner creative, as well as an excuse to hit the outdoors.

MasterChef first crossed my mind after watching the Australian 2014 series with Beck. We got really into it, and that helped a lot with improving my knowledge of and experimentation with different techniques. Beck and I would wander the markets together in the weekends and pick up whatever was in season. I'd then whip our purchases up into something for her family.

We joked that if there happened to be another season of *MasterChef New Zealand* I should give it a go. So it was only natural that when I saw the application form I filled it out. I never entered *MasterChef* thinking I'd win – I just wanted to continue to learn and maybe get some confirmation that I'm not a bad cook.

Fast forward a few months and I got an apron with my audition dish of venison with autumn veges. I thought I had made it! The apron alone was all the confirmation I needed that I was a decent cook – I could have gone home happy then no matter what. In saying that, I decided to work as hard as I could for as long as I could, so that if I did go home it wouldn't be because of a lack of effort. The rest, as they say, is history. I made it into the house, then to the top 10, then the top six, then the top four (and the trip to Dubai), and at last to the final, pipping Leo at the post to win *MasterChef* 2015.

It wasn't all highs though; there were some moments of serious lows. On top of being away from loved ones, routine, the bush and

Cooking became a way of releasing my inner creative, as well as an excuse to hit the outdoors.

the water, there was also the pressure to perform every day to the best of my abilities against some outstanding cooks. Many a time I had to pick myself up from a disappointing day in the kitchen, dust myself off, remind myself of my decision to work hard and get back to it. Beck, my family, Beck's family and the boys were great with their encouragement during these times and I'm really thankful for that.

One of the greatest things to come out of *MasterChef* has been the relationships I've built with fellow foodies – not just the ones in the house, but also from the auditions. To all of you, thank you for being who you are, thank you for sharing this incredible experience with me and thank you for creating an environment of sharing both knowledge and, of course, food. Thanks must also go to the judges and to the team who put *MasterChef* together. Josh, Mark and Al, you three guys are amazing chefs and even better people. Thanks for taking the time to invest in me, pushing me when I needed it and encouraging me to find who I am as a cook. I learnt so much from you three and am incredibly grateful. To Darryl, Simon and the Imagination Television team, thank you for creating a platform that has changed my life. I'll forever be thankful for the work you put in to making the show what it was.

Be blessed,
Tim Read
MasterChef New Zealand Winner 2015

pork

Smoky Barbecue Ribs with Crispy Potatoes and Slaw

Who doesn't love ribs? Granted they probably aren't the dish for a first date, a wedding or a funeral, but any other time they are completely suitable. These little delights are roasted first, then grilled with my homemade barbecue sauce. The key here is to allow the ribs to char just a little on the outside when they're on the grill. It'll add to the authentic smoky flavour, which is what we all love about ribs. I've kept the sides pretty classic: crispy potatoes to mop up the barbecue sauce and a slaw to keep Mum happy.

Preheat the oven to 150°C.

Combine the paprika, fennel, cumin, chilli powder, salt and pepper. Drizzle the ribs with a little oil and rub over the spices. Place the ribs on an oven tray in between 2 pieces of tin foil and bake in the oven for 3 hours.

Cook the potatoes in a saucepan of boiling salted water for 10 minutes or until soft. Drain and shake around in a colander to roughen up the potatoes so they'll take up more oil when you roast them. Return to the saucepan to dry out in the residual heat.

Heat the barbecue grill to high.

Take the ribs out of the oven and crank the temperature up to 200°C. Toss the potatoes on an oven tray with the butter and roast in the oven until crispy. Turn and toss the potatoes every 10 minutes for a total of 40 minutes.

Baste the ribs in the barbecue sauce and grill on the barbecue, basting often, for 5–7 minutes each side.

In a large bowl, toss the cabbage, carrots and parsley together with the mayo. Divvy up the potatoes and slaw. I don't think I need to tell you what to do with the ribs – dig in!

Preparation time: 40 minutes

Cooking time: 40 minutes

Feeds: 4

BARBECUE RIBS

2 teaspoons paprika

½ teaspoon ground fennel

½ teaspoon ground cumin

1 teaspoon chilli powder

1 teaspoon salt

1 teaspoon black pepper

1kg ribs

1 cup barbecue sauce (see page 168)

CRISPY POTATOES

500g potatoes, peeled

50g butter

SLAW

½ cabbage, finely sliced

2 large carrots, peeled and finely sliced

handful of fresh flat-leaf parsley, finely chopped

½ cup Tim's mayo (see page 150)

Confit Pork Belly with Spicy Fig Sauce

Preparation time: 24 hours	
Cooking time: 5 hours	
Feeds: 4	

PORK BELLY

3–4 star anise

4 cloves garlic

1 teaspoon black peppercorns

½ cup salt

¼ cup honey

4 cups water

1 fennel bulb, roughly chopped (fronds reserved for garnish)

1kg pork belly, skin on

1 litre olive oil

SPICY FIG SAUCE

8 dried figs, roughly chopped

3 red chillies, roughly chopped

1 tablespoon fennel seeds

1½ cups water

¼ cup caster sugar, plus extra for blowtorching

1 tablespoon fish sauce

3 tablespoons soy sauce

This recipe does take a very long time if you do it properly, but for me there is no other pork belly recipe that comes remotely close. The saltiness of the meat, the sweetness of the confit crackling and the spice in the fig sauce is all just awesome. Most of the prep and cooking for this one can be done the day before, or even up to a week before. I recommend starting the day before you intend to eat the pork belly. I have made the recipe all in a day, but it involved a pretty early start then stumbling back to bed. The pork is perfect with a crisp summer salad with fennel and lime.

Note: To perforate the skin, I use a bunch of skewers taped together to stab the skin rather than crisscrossing it with a knife. I find this technique gives a much more even crisp on the skin.

If you don't have a blowtorch to finish the crackling, whack it in the oven under the grill – just keep a good eye on it as it won't take long at all!

Combine the star anise, garlic, peppercorns, salt, honey, water and fennel in a large stockpot. Bring to a simmer and cook until the salt has completely dissolved. Chill the brine in the fridge until cooled.

Place the pork belly in a zip-lock bag and pour enough brine into the bag to submerge the pork. Place the bag in an oven tray and leave in the fridge for 6 hours. Make sure the pork belly is fully submerged at all times.

Preheat the oven to 110°C.

Take the pork belly out of the brine, clean off any spices that might be stuck to it and pat dry with paper towels. Place the pork skin side down in a small oven tray – the better the fit of the tray, the less fat you'll need to confit the pork.

Pour the olive oil into a saucepan and heat it gently for 5 minutes over a medium heat. Pour over the pork belly, ensuring it is covered. Cover the tray with tin foil and cook the pork in the oven for 4 hours until very tender and easy to pierce with a fork.

Carefully remove the pork belly from the tray (the oil will be hot) and place on a chopping board, skin side up. Using a bunch of skewers, pierce the skin all over, making sure you don't push too hard and ruin the fat layer under the skin. (When it's cool, I strain and then store the used olive oil in an old milk container for the next time I make this recipe.)

Place the pork belly skin side down in a flat-bottomed dish, cover with plastic wrap, then place another flat-bottomed plate on top of the pork. Chuck it back in the fridge with a couple of cans on top. Keep the

Recipe continued over page . . .

pork chilled in the fridge for at least 10 hours, or up to a week.

When you're ready to finish cooking the pork, make the spicy fig sauce. Place the dried figs, chillies, fennel seeds and water in a small saucepan over a medium heat. Simmer for 10 minutes. Add the sugar, fish sauce and soy sauce to the pan and continue to simmer until a syrupy consistency. Strain the sauce through a sieve and return to the pan to keep warm.

To finish cooking the pork belly, take about 2 tablespoons of the solidified pork fat from the dish (or use oil) and add it to a large frying pan over a low heat. Carefully lay the pork belly skin side down in the pan and cover with a lid or some tin foil, leaving a small opening. The skin will pop, explode and spit hot fat, but you want a little steam to escape. Cook for 15–20 minutes on a low heat, then remove the lid and cook for a further 5–20 minutes. Yes, a bit of a difference in cooking time but this depends on the thickness of the skin – just keep checking it every 5 minutes until it's all crispy.

Transfer the pork belly to a chopping board, skin side up. Cover the skin with an even layer of caster sugar, enough so you can't see the skin through the sugar. Caramelise the sugar with a blowtorch until completely melted and browned. Leave the caramel to harden for a couple of minutes. Flip the pork so it's skin side down and cut into strips.

Line up the strips of pork belly on a plate, drizzle with the spicy fig sauce, top with the fennel fronds and tuck in. You won't want pork belly any other way ever again!

Pork, Plum and Kale Salad

Preparation time: 30 minutes

Cooking time: 35 minutes

Feeds: 4

1 tablespoon fennel seeds

600g pork tenderloins

4 tablespoons olive oil

salt and pepper

¼ cup almonds

4 plums, cut into eighths

¼ cup apple cider vinegar

1 tablespoon Dijon mustard

big bunch of kale, large stalks removed and leaves finely sliced

I first cooked this recipe with Beck, who was a big part of the team supporting me as I entered *MasterChef*. It was the middle of winter and I was sick of being cooped up inside so I convinced her that we should cook this over an open fire. Looking back, I just laugh at the fact we froze for a few hours, all for the sake of having a meal outside — it was totally worth it though. I love the ruggedness of this meal (yes, kale is popular now but I'll always think it's food for cattle). I try to use pork loin that I've shot myself as the strong flavours of the plum and vinaigrette stand up to the gamey-ness of the meat.

Preheat the oven to 220°C. Place an oven tray inside to heat up.

Crush the fennel seeds to a powder with a mortar and pestle.

Coat the pork in 2 tablespoons of the olive oil, then sprinkle evenly with the ground fennel and season with salt and pepper. Place the pork in the preheated tray and roast for 10 minutes.

Place the almonds in a separate roasting tray and roast for 8 minutes. Remove from the oven and allow to cool. Then crush and set aside for serving.

Flip the pork over, reduce the temperature to 200°C and roast for a further 10–15 minutes or until cooked through. Remove from the oven and allow to rest under tin foil for 10 minutes. When rested, slice the tenderloins.

Drizzle the plums with a tablespoon of the olive oil and season with salt and pepper. Heat a saucepan over a medium-high heat, then fry the plum slices for 2 minutes each side until caramelised. Set aside.

Whisk the remaining tablespoon of the olive oil together with the apple cider vinegar and Dijon mustard. Season with salt and pepper to taste.

Toss the kale with the vinaigrette and place in a large serving bowl. Top with the plums, almonds and sliced pork tenderloin.

Pulled Pork Sliders

Preparation time: 30 minutes plus marinating time

Cooking time: 3 hours

Feeds: 4

---

1 pork shoulder

Carolina rub mix (see page 164)

5 red apples

2 large brown onions, cut into roughly 1cm-thick slices

3 cups apple cider

½ green cabbage, finely sliced

1 cup Tim's mayo (see page 150)

100g chipotle chillies, roughly chopped

25g butter

8 slider buns (see page 156 or use storebought)

These bad boys have really grown in popularity over the last few years and for good reason. Sliders are delicious, feed a crowd pretty easily and test your patience more than your cooking skill. The rub tastes best with a little time so try prepping it on a Wednesday night in time for Saturday or Sunday dinner — it will work with just a few hours in the fridge but the flavour will not be as pronounced. In New Zealand chipotle chillies are usually only found in a small can, somewhere near the pickles aisle. They are amazing and I recommend using them, although you can substitute them with straight chipotle sauce. I like using wild pork shoulder for this recipe, which I get when I'm out hunting — the simmering cider underneath ensures the fatless wild meat doesn't dry out.

Note: The slider bun recipe on page 156 is unreal. Give it a go to get the full homemade experience.

Rub the pork shoulder with Carolina rub mix and cover with plastic wrap. Leave in the fridge for 24 hours or 3–4 days if possible. Remove from the fridge 1 hour before cooking to bring up to room temperature. If you are making the slider buns, start the dough-making process when you get the pork out of the fridge; that should mean everything is ready at about the same time.

Preheat the oven to 200°C.

Cut 3 of the apples into roughly 1cm-thick slices. Cover the bottom of an oven tray big enough to hold the pork shoulder with the apple and onion slices. Place the pork on top of the onion and apple and pour in the cider. Cover the tray with tin foil, sealing tightly, and place in the oven. Immediately reduce the temperature to 150°C and cook the pork for 2½ hours, turning it over halfway through. The pork should be tender and pull apart easily.

Peel, core and cut the remaining apples into matchsticks. Combine with the cabbage in a large bowl and stir through 3 tablespoons of the mayo. Refrigerate till required.

Blend the remaining mayo and chipotle chillies till a smooth and even colour. Season to taste with salt and pepper, then refrigerate.

Once the pork has cooked, pour three-quarters of the pan juices into a saucepan and reduce by two-thirds over a medium-high heat for 20 minutes. Allow the meat to rest under tin foil for 20 minutes. Whisk the butter into the reduced sauce and remove from the heat. Shred the pork meat, combine with the sauce and mix well.

Take your slider buns, smear with a liberal amount of chipotle mayo, top with some pork and then the slaw. Whack the lid on top of the slider and get stuck in.

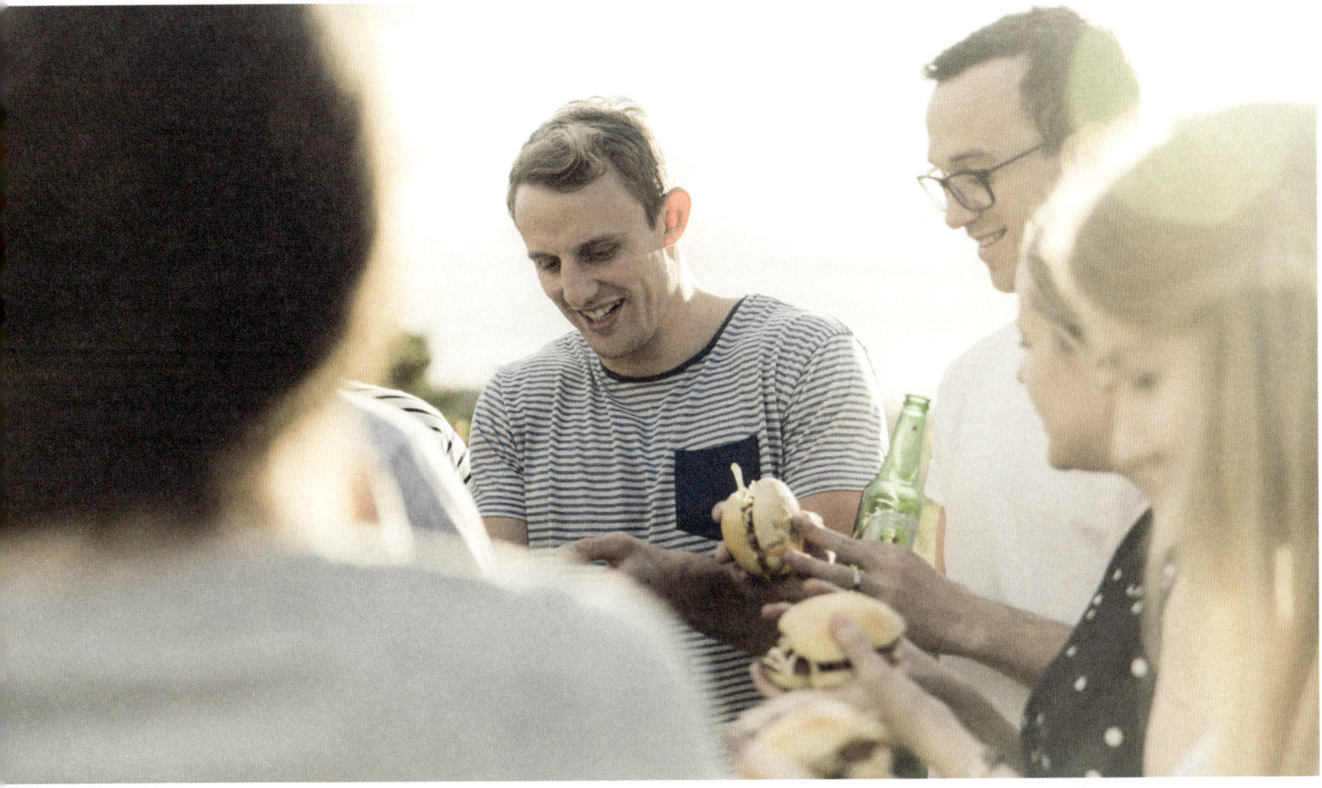

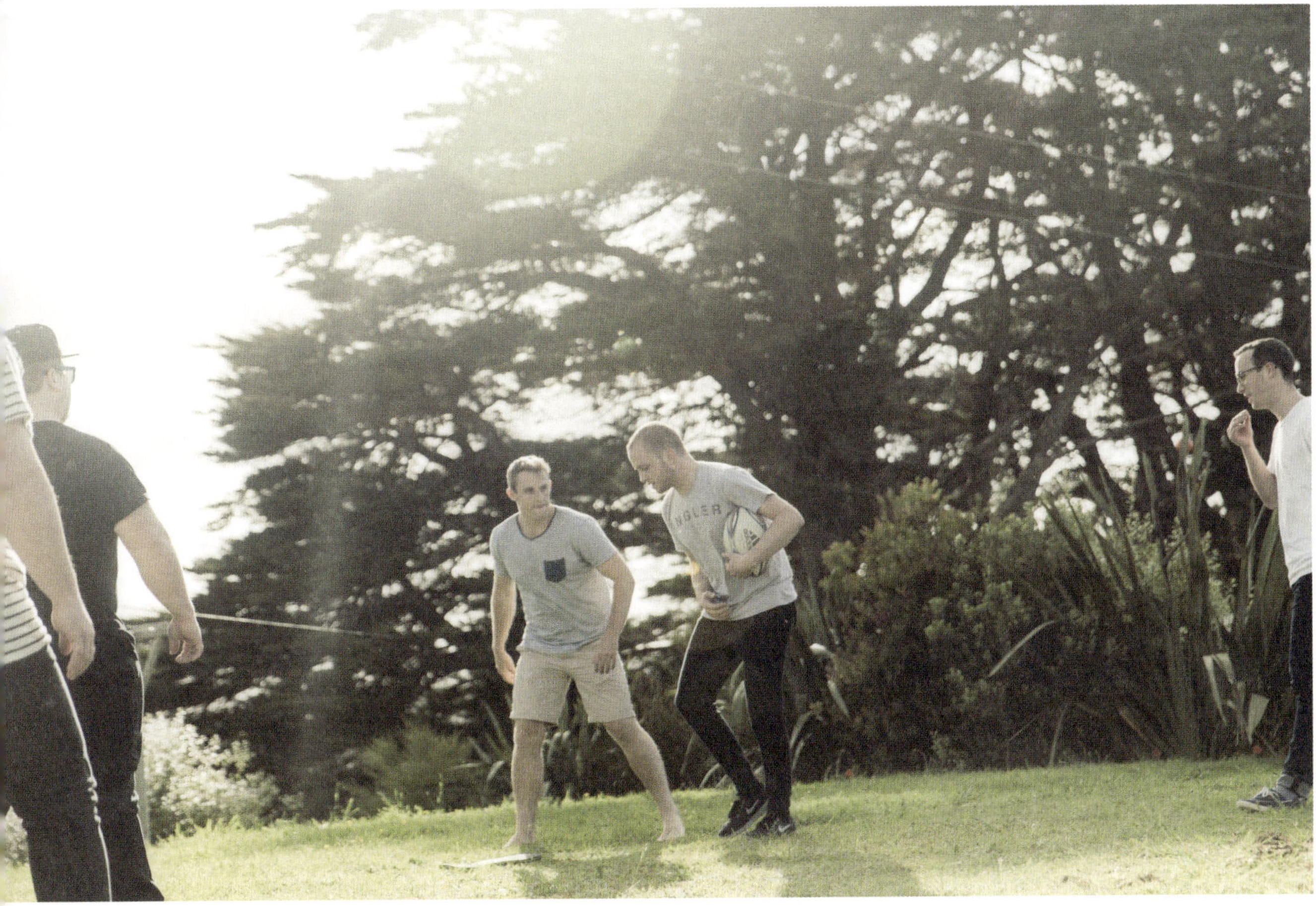

Pork Enchiladas with Chilli Corn

My mouth drools when I think of these cheesy enchiladas; on a good day I'd give the whole lot a run for their money. If you don't like your enchiladas spicy you can trade out some of the chilli for a similar amount of red capsicum, and remember you can always add more sour cream at the other end to tone down the dish. Let me know when you're serving these beauties with the roasted sweet corn, and I'll be over for dinner!

Preparation time:	1 hour
Cooking time:	30 minutes
Feeds:	4

ENCHILADAS

2 tablespoons oil

1 large brown onion, roughly diced

3 cloves garlic, roughly diced

2 tablespoons plain flour

1 tablespoon ground cumin

2 tablespoons smoked paprika

2 teaspoons ground cinnamon

2 red chillies, diced

500g pork mince

250g chorizo, diced

400g can tomatoes

2 cups chicken stock

¼ cup fresh oregano, roughly chopped

salt and pepper

8 tortillas (see page 174)

150g cheddar cheese, grated

2 jalapeños, diced (optional)

CHILLI CORN

50g butter

2 red chillies, finely diced

4 corn cobs, husks removed

sour cream to serve

lime wedges to serve

Heat the oil in a large saucepan over a medium-high heat. Add the onion and garlic, and fry for 7–8 minutes or until they begin to caramelise. Stir in the flour, cumin, paprika and cinnamon and cook for 5 minutes.

Add the chillies to the pan with the pork mince and chorizo. Cook until the mince is well browned. Add the tomatoes, stock and oregano, then season well with salt and pepper. Bring to a simmer then leave to simmer for 30 minutes.

While the mince is simmering, make the chilli butter for the corn. Partially melt the butter in the microwave. In a bowl, combine the chillies and butter with a little salt and pepper. Refrigerate, covered, until ready to use.

Preheat the oven to 190°C.

Spread the corn with a good dollop of the chilli butter. Wrap the cobs in tin foil and roast in the oven for 30 minutes. Remove the corn from the foil.

Using a slotted spoon, place some mince mixture into the middle of each tortilla (don't use it all). Roll them up and place all eight in a baking dish. Spoon some of the mince sauce over the enchiladas and top with the cheese and jalapeños (if using). Bake in the oven for 25 minutes, then remove and allow to cool slightly while the corn finishes cooking.

Give each person a couple of enchiladas, top with sour cream and place some lime wedges on the side. Throw around the corn cobs so they're smeared with the chilli butter.

Bacon Hock, Cress and Pine Nut Ravioli

I was never going to write a cookbook without bacon being a major ingredient in at least one recipe, so here it is: my tribute to bacon. Smoked bacon with peppery watercress, woody pine nuts and the nuttiness of Beaufort – you can just tell this meal is going to be epic, so enough said. If you can't get your hands on Beaufort, you can use Gruyère instead.

Ravioli can seem a little fiddly if it's your first time making them but the key is to keep the sheets of pasta nice and long and to have enough bench space to work on. That way you can bash out the lot in one simple production line. Go easy on the salt with this one – the sauce gets pretty salty from the cheese, and the hock has salt in it too. I recommend doing most of the seasoning at the table.

Preparation time: 2 hours

Cooking time: 15 minutes

Feeds: 4

1 smoked bacon hock

3 cups apple cider

1 cup pine nuts

3 cups watercress leaves

¼ cup cream

50g Beaufort cheese, grated

pasta dough (see page 154)

1 egg, beaten

freshly ground black pepper

Place the bacon hock and apple cider in a large stockpot. Simmer for 2 hours or until the meat pulls easily away from the bone. Reserve the cooking juices. Remove the meat from the hock and discard the bones and skin. Shred the meat with two forks and set aside to cool.

Toast the pine nuts in a dry frying pan over a high heat for 3–4 minutes. Place in a food processor with 2 cups of the watercress leaves and the meat. Pulse 10–15 times until the mixture resembles a rough paste.

Take 1 cup of the reserved cooking liquid and pour into a saucepan over a medium-high heat. Reduce by half, then whisk in the cream, followed by the cheese. Keep warm.

Bring a large saucepan of salted water to a rolling boil.

Divide the pasta dough in half and roll out each piece on the thinnest setting possible on the pasta machine so you have 2 separate sheets of the same length. Take 1 sheet and lay it out flat on a lightly floured bench. Using a ravioli cutter or sharp knife, lightly score the outline of your desired shapes – 5cm square is roughly a good size. Brush the beaten egg over the pasta sheet where the filling will go. Place a spoonful of filling in the middle of each shape, top with the second sheet of pasta and press round the edges to seal, then cut out the ravioli.

Cook the ravioli, in batches of about five, for about 6 minutes or until the pasta is al dente. Scoop the cooked ravioli out with a slotted spoon and toss in the warm cheese sauce.

Serve on a plate with a spoonful of sauce, a few extra watercress leaves, a pinch of salt and a grind of pepper.

Pancetta, Mushroom, Artichoke Heart and Olive Pizza

Preparation time: 50 minutes

Cooking time: 8–10 minutes

Makes: 4 medium-sized pizzas

1 batch pizza dough (see page 152)

3 tablespoons tapenade paste

3 tablespoons tomato paste

100g pancetta, shredded

50g oyster mushrooms, quartered

4 artichoke hearts, quartered

100g buffalo mozzarella, torn

truffle-infused olive oil to drizzle

salt and pepper

flat-leaf parsley to garnish

This guy is an adaptation from the pizza night we had in the *MasterChef* house. The house was such a good learning experience for me and forced me to branch out and try different things — a hearty vegetarian pizza is something I wouldn't have usually made, but I loved it. I did think at the time, though, that all it needed was a little pancetta, so I've snuck that in here. The little bit of truffle oil complements the artichoke heart and mushroom so well.

Prepare the pizza dough following the instructions on page 152.

Preheat the oven to 190°C.

Combine the tapenade and tomato paste then spread over the pizza bases. Scatter the pancetta, mushrooms, artichoke hearts and mozzarella all over the pizza. Drizzle with a little truffle-infused oil.

Pop the pizzas on a baking tray and cook in the oven till the bases are crispy on the bottom (7–10 minutes). Remove from the oven, and allow pizzas to cool for 3 minutes before seasoning with salt and pepper. Garnish with parsley. Slice and get stuck in.

beef

Bone Marrow with Salsa Verde and Crusty Bread

Preparation time: 5 minutes

Cooking time: 20 minutes

Feeds: 4

BONE MARROW

6–8 marrow bones, cut lengthways

3 tablespoons celery seeds

salt and pepper

SALSA VERDE

2 shallots, finely diced

1 cup finely sliced fresh flat-leaf parsley

¼ cup Kalamata olives, finely diced

juice of 1 large lemon

2 tablespoons olive oil

good-quality crusty white bread (ciabatta or the like) to serve

This wee gem is perfect as a starter or for a lazy weekend platter. Bone marrow isn't something we eat a lot of here in New Zealand, but with the amount of beef we produce we should. Marrow bones are occasionally available at supermarkets but can be bought at any good butcher — you might just have to ask for them. To be honest, that's the hardest part of this dish. The rest is super simple, super tasty and will leave you wishing you'd bought more bones. I know the salsa verde isn't a classic version but I like the heavy flavours of the Kalamata olives with the richness of the marrow. I'm sure you'll agree.

Preheat the oven to 220°C.

Place the marrow bones in a large oven tray, marrow side up. Sprinkle with the celery seeds and season liberally with salt and pepper. Place in the oven for 15–20 minutes or until the marrow is soft and comes away from the bone but is not melted.

While the marrow is cooking, make the salsa verde. Place the shallots, parsley and olives in a bowl. Stir through the lemon juice and olive oil. Season well and set aside.

Once the marrow has cooked, remove the bones from the oven and let them cool.

Spread some bone marrow on slices of crusty bread and top with salsa verde. Serve immediately.

Skirt Steak Salad Wraps with Korean Chilli Dressing

Pretty soon after I left home, Mum started working for a weight-loss company and got hooked on healthy food. Going home for a fuel-up changed a lot over that time. All of a sudden those much-loved pasta bakes turned into salads, and veges appeared in my bacon and egg pie – I wasn't always impressed, but I was a hungry student so I ate it with a smile. One little beaut that Mum introduced me to is the lettuce-leaf wrap. I love the freshness the crunchy lettuce brings to this dish.

This is one of those meals that is so, so simple; if you have nothing organised by 5.30 at night, you can whip it together super quick. It'll leave the troops with a smile on their dial and a full belly. If you wanted some, a few roast potatoes wouldn't go amiss here.

Preparation time: 30 minutes

Cooking time: 10 minutes.

Feeds: 4

SKIRT STEAK

800g skirt steak

4 tablespoons soy sauce

1 teaspoon caster sugar

4 tablespoons sesame oil

salt and pepper

DRESSING

1 thumbnail-sized piece of ginger, peeled and chopped

2 cloves garlic, chopped

2 red chillies, roughly chopped

1 tablespoon tomato paste

2 tablespoons lime juice

2 tablespoons rice wine vinegar

1 tablespoon fish sauce

1 tablespoon chilli flakes

1 tablespoon honey

50g butter

TO ASSEMBLE

2 iceberg lettuces, leaves separated and washed

1 small daikon, peeled and grated

2 large carrots, peeled and cut into thin strips

5 spring onions, finely sliced

To marinate the steak, combine the soy sauce, caster sugar and sesame oil in a large bowl. Coat the meat well in the marinade and season with salt and pepper. Set aside until ready to cook.

Toss the ginger, garlic and chilli into a food processor. Add the tomato paste, lime juice, vinegar, fish sauce and chilli flakes, and blend to a smooth paste. Transfer this mixture to a frying pan with the honey. Place over a medium heat and cook for 2 minutes. Add the butter 1 teaspoon at a time, whisking constantly until all the butter is incorporated into the sauce. Remove from the heat and set aside.

Separate the lettuce leaves and wash them well. Drain on paper towels until ready to serve.

Heat a frying pan with a drizzle of olive oil to medium-high heat. Remove the steak from the marinade and season once again with salt and pepper. Cook the steak until medium-rare, about 3–4 minutes each side, then remove from the pan and rest under tin foil for 8 minutes. Slice the rested steak into 1cm-thick strips.

Take a couple of slices of steak and place them inside a lettuce leaf, top with the vegetables and a solid serving of dressing. Roll up and enjoy.

Spiced Brisket with Texan Salad

Preparation time: 24 hours to 3 days (depending on marinating time)

Cooking time: 4½ hours

Feeds: 5

TEXAN RUB

2 tablespoons chilli powder

2 tablespoons cayenne pepper

2 tablespoons ground black pepper

1 tablespoon salt

1 tablespoon garlic powder

SPICED BRISKET

2kg beef brisket

1 large brown onion, roughly chopped

4 cloves garlic, roughly chopped

2 cups beef stock

TEXAN SALAD

500g baby potatoes, scrubbed

5 slices bacon

1 red onion, roughly sliced

1 tablespoon cumin seeds

bunch of fresh coriander, finely chopped

2 red chillies, finely chopped

¼ cup olive oil

1 tablespoon red wine vinegar

salt and pepper

It's crazy how the price of meat now is based on popularity and convenience rather than quality. Thankfully for my wallet, brisket is not the latest thing (I usually get my 2-kilogram cut for under $20). I'm the first to admit that, compared with whacking a steak on the barbecue and eating it 10 minutes later, brisket is definitely not convenient. However, when it comes to taste, you will be hard pressed to beat a quality piece of brisket, with all the marbling of fat adding so much flavour and juiciness to the meat. With a bit of a kick added by the spicy rub and the baby potatoes with chilli and bacon, this meal on a summer evening will go down in memory for a long time.

Combine all the Texan rub ingredients and mix well. Store in an airtight container until you're ready to prepare the brisket.

Take the Texan rub and apply all over the beef brisket, ensuring you coat it well. Cover the brisket with plastic wrap and pop in the fridge overnight or for up to 3 days.

Preheat the oven to 130°C.

Put the brisket into a deep oven tray along with the onion and garlic. Pour in the stock and cover tightly with tin foil. Roast in the oven for 4½ hours. Check the fluid levels after 3 hours and add more stock if you need to. After 4½ hours remove the beef from the tray; it should be very tender and lightly pink on the inside. Place the brisket on a chopping board, under tin foil, to rest for 20 minutes.

Cook the potatoes in boiling salted water for 20–25 minutes or until tender. Drain and cool to room temperature. Halve the potatoes and set aside.

Cook the bacon in a frying pan over medium heat until crispy. Remove the bacon but leave the fat in the pan and turn the heat down to low. Cook the onion in the bacon fat until lightly caramelised. Dice the bacon.

Toast the cumin seeds in a small, dry frying pan on medium heat until fragrant.

Place the potatoes in a large bowl with the bacon, onion, cumin seeds, coriander and chillies. Pour over the olive oil and red wine vinegar, then season well with salt and pepper.

Cut the slow-cooked brisket into slices roughly 1cm thick and serve on a big platter with the Texan salad.

More to share
means more
memories made.

Roast Beef with Cauliflower and Horseradish Mash and Gravy

I would almost cook roast beef just to use it in sandwiches. In my eyes it's the best sort of roast. Cauliflower is having something of a comeback at the moment – you see it popping up everywhere, cut into steaks, raw as a garnish or as charred florets. I've used it here as a mash with beef's best mate: horseradish. A cauliflower mash is about as simple as it comes and the light, almost nutty flavour gives this dish a cool, earthy feel. It wouldn't be a roast without a good gravy so there's one of those too.

Preparation time: 20 minutes

Cooking time: 40 minutes (depending on size of roast)

Feeds: 4

ROAST BEEF

2 tablespoons olive oil

1 sirloin of beef

salt and pepper

handful of fresh rosemary

handful of fresh thyme

CAULIFLOWER AND HORSERADISH MASH

1 large head cauliflower, cut into florets

½ cup sour cream

2 tablespoons horseradish cream

100g feta

salt and pepper

GRAVY

1 cup red wine

2 cups beef stock

Preheat the oven to 180°C.

Rub the olive oil all over the beef and season well with salt and pepper. Heat an oven tray over a high heat on the stove top then add the beef, fat side down, to render out some of the fat. After 3–4 minutes, turn the beef and sear it for a couple of minutes on all sides. Turn the beef fat side up, throw in the rosemary and thyme and pop in the oven to roast for 15 minutes per 500g for medium-rare (or about 20 minutes for medium). Once cooked to your liking, remove the meat from the pan and rest under tin foil for 10–15 minutes.

Place the cauliflower florets in a saucepan of boiling salted water, and cook with the lid on for 10 minutes until the cauliflower is very soft. Drain, then return the cauliflower to the pan, add the sour cream, horseradish and feta, and mash together. Season with salt and pepper, and keep warm.

To make the gravy, pour out any excess fat from the oven tray and discard the herbs. Place the tray over a high heat and when it begins to sizzle, add the red wine. Allow the wine to boil and reduce until almost evaporated, then add the beef stock and reduce to a syrup consistency (about 15 minutes). Pour the gravy into a boat and get ready to carve the meat.

Carve the beef, serve the cauliflower mash in a large bowl and get stuck in. Cover EVERYTHING in gravy!

Schnitzel Dogs with Tomato, Mozzarella and Basil

Preparation time: 30 minutes

Cooking time: 10 minutes

Feeds: 4

CRUMBED VEAL

500g veal schnitzel

2 eggs

2 tablespoons milk

1 cup plain flour

salt and pepper

2 cups breadcrumbs

vegetable oil to cook

TO ASSEMBLE

4 hotdog rolls or slider buns
(see page 156)

butter for spreading

mayo for spreading

4 tomatoes, sliced

100g buffalo mozzarella, sliced

handful of fresh basil leaves

Richard from *MasterChef* introduced me to veal. Being a butcher, he knows what he's on about when it comes to meat, so when he told me to try it I didn't muck around. Now I'm a fan. Veal's smoothness, almost sweetness, is unreal and when I was thinking of a way to use beef in a bun it immediately came to mind. Beautiful crumbed veal, paired with a Caprese salad in a crispy bun with mayo – it's pretty good. Don't skimp on the buffalo mozzarella – it might be a little pricier than the stuff from cows but it has a completely different flavour.

Cut the veal schnitzel into 2cm-wide strips. Place the eggs and milk in a bowl and whisk to combine. Put the flour in another bowl and season with salt and pepper. Place the breadcrumbs in a third bowl. Dredge each veal strip in flour, then egg mixture, then through the breadcrumbs. Place the coated strips on a plate and, when they are all done, pop them in the fridge for 15 minutes. This will help the coating to stick.

Cover the base of a large frying pan with vegetable oil and place over a medium-high heat. When the oil is hot, cook the schnitzel strips in batches until brown and crispy on each side, roughly 3–4 minutes. Drain the cooked strips on paper towels as you go.

Preheat the oven grill.

Cut the buns in half and spread some butter on each half. Grill the buns until crispy.

To assemble, spread some mayo on the buns. Chuck in a few schnitzel strips, top with tomato, mozzarella and basil, and dig in!

Chilli Con Carne with Guasacaca and Corn Muffins

Preparation time: 20 minutes

Cooking time: 1½ hours

Feeds: 4

CHILLI CON CARNE

800g beef chuck roast, roughly diced

1 tablespoon olive oil

1 large brown onion, diced

3 cloves garlic, crushed

1 red capsicum, diced

1½ teaspoons smoked paprika

1½ teaspoons ground cumin

½ teaspoon cayenne pepper

1 tablespoon cornflour

400g can red kidney beans

3 small tomatoes, diced

2 tablespoons tomato paste

1 cup beef stock

salt and pepper

CORN MUFFINS

110g butter

1 cup plain flour

1 cup cornmeal

¼ cup caster sugar

1 tablespoon baking powder

1 teaspoon salt

2 eggs

1 cup buttermilk

1 cup corn kernels

100g cheddar cheese, grated

fresh coriander leaves to serve

guasacaca (see page 160) to serve

I love coming home on a slightly cooler spring evening to a dish like chilli con carne – it will warm you through, yet its flavours let you know that summer is on the way. Top it off with guasacaca, my new favourite guacamole alternative, fresh coriander and some fluffy corn muffins for dipping, and you'll have a family hit. Double the ingredients if you like and freeze both the chilli and the muffins for a day when you can't be bothered cooking.

Season the steak with salt. Heat the olive oil in a large saucepan over a medium-high heat. Throw in the onion, garlic and capsicum, and lightly caramelise for 4–5 minutes. Remove the vegetables from the pan. Add the steak to the pan and brown on all sides (depending on the size of the pan, you may have to do this in batches).

Return all the ingredients to the pan and add the smoked paprika, cumin, cayenne pepper, cornflour, kidney beans, tomatoes, tomato paste and beef stock. Season with salt and pepper. Bring up to a gentle simmer, then turn the heat to low and simmer with the lid on for 1½ hours or until the meat is tender.

Preheat the oven to 180°C. Grease a 12-mould muffin tray with olive oil and lightly dust with flour.

Melt the butter in the microwave, then allow to cool.

Sift the flour, cornmeal, caster sugar, baking powder and salt into a large bowl.

Beat the eggs in a separate bowl, then add the buttermilk, corn kernels and melted butter, and stir. Combine the wet and dry ingredients until well mixed, add the cheese and combine again. Spoon the mixture into the muffin trays and bake for 30 minutes. Rest for 10 minutes before removing the muffins from the tray.

When the chilli con carne is cooked, shred the beef with two forks. Spoon liberal amounts of chilli into each serving bowl, and top with guasacaca and coriander. Dip the corn muffins into the chilli.

Beef Shin Cobbler

Preparation time: 30 minutes

Cooking time: 2 hours 10 minutes

Feeds: 4

BEEF SHIN STEW

1kg beef shin (reserve marrow from bone)

25g butter

salt and pepper

½ cup plain flour

2 slices bacon, diced

1 large brown onion, diced

4 cloves garlic, diced

1 celery stalk, diced

1 large carrot, peeled and diced

50g button mushrooms

350ml beef stock

350ml red wine

2 bay leaves

COBBLER

2⅔ cups self-raising flour

200g butter

3 tablespoons chopped fresh flat-leaf parsley

salt and pepper

3 tablespoons water

juice of 1 lemon

TO SERVE

fresh flat-leaf parsley

I love a good cobbler. While I was away in Dubai for *MasterChef* I began to wonder why I couldn't make a savoury cobbler . . . I found myself in a little bit of a rabbit hole trying to figure out what a good recipe would be, and what I wanted it to be like. I think I've finally stumbled on something I'm pretty happy with: the dough is not so light that it just falls apart when soaked in liquid but not so doughy that it can't be eaten with a spoon.

Preheat the oven to 180°C.

Remove the marrow from the beef shin by scooping it out with a teaspoon. Dice the meat. Place the butter and marrow in a casserole dish or large ovenproof frying pan and place on the stove top over a medium-high heat until the butter begins to brown. Season the beef with salt and pepper, then toss in the flour. Add to the dish or pan and brown the beef with the bacon. Remove the meat from the dish and set aside.

Add the onion, garlic, celery and carrot to the dish and cook until softened. Remove the vegetables from the dish and set aside.

Toss in the whole mushrooms and lightly brown. Return all the vegetables and meat to the dish, then add the stock, wine and bay leaves. Bring to the boil, then cover with a lid or tin foil, and cook in the oven for 1 hour and 20 minutes.

When the stew has reached the 1 hour mark, make the cobbler. Combine the self-raising flour, butter and parsley in a bowl, rubbing in the butter. Season with salt and pepper. Add the water and lemon juice and use a fork to mix into a dough. Lightly flour the bench, and roll out the dough to about 0.5cm thickness and cut out 10 circles using a cookie cutter.

Remove the stew from the oven and season with salt and pepper. Place the cobblers on the stew round the perimeter of the casserole dish. Cook for a further 50 minutes with the lid off until the top of the cobbler is golden brown. Serve with a sprinkle of parsley.

chicken

Garlic Butter Chicken Salad with Cranberry Balsamic Sauce

Preparation time: 30 minutes

Cooking time: 1 hour

Feeds: 4

1 whole chicken

100g butter, at room temperature

4 cloves garlic, finely chopped

salt and pepper

5 tablespoons cranberry jelly

1 tablespoon balsamic vinegar

2 cos lettuces, leaves roughly torn

150g goat's feta, crumbled

¾ cup walnuts, roughly chopped

This recipe takes me back to one of the first dinner parties I had with a group of university mates. My good friends the Milnes had me and some mates over and served us this buttery, garlicky barbecued chicken by the truckload with a selection of beautiful salads. This meal sticks clearly in my mind because it was in the middle of exam study, and being able to pause for a moment with good people and good food helped us no end to keep trucking on. I love what food can do for people – much more than fill a belly – so this recipe is a nod to those memories and the ones to come.

Note: This recipe can be cooked two ways. Here, I've given the instructions for the oven, but cooking it on the barbecue is just beautiful. To do so, place the chicken skin side down on the barbecue, cranked up to full heat, and cook until the skin is crispy (10–15 minutes). Carefully flip the chicken so it's skin side up, turn the heat down to medium and close the lid or cover with an oven tray. Cook for a further 30 minutes or until the juices run clear.

Preheat the oven to 190°C.

To butterfly the chicken, place it breast side down on a chopping board. Cut along both sides of the backbone from end to end with a sharp pair of scissors and remove the backbone. Flip the chicken, and open it up like a book. Press firmly on the breasts with your palm to flatten.

Mix the butter and garlic together well. Create a little space between the chicken meat and the skin with your fingers and squeeze some butter into the gap. You can then squish the butter all over the meat. Make sure there's a lot over the breasts, where the meat is more likely to dry out. Season the chicken all over with salt and pepper.

Place the chicken in a roasting tray and pop in the oven for an hour, or until the juices run clear. The skin should crisp and brown up nicely. Remove the chicken and rest for 10 minutes under tin foil.

Combine the cranberry jelly and balsamic vinegar in a small saucepan over a medium heat. Cook the mixture, stirring regularly, until the intense acid flavour of the vinegar is cooked out (8–10 minutes). Taste the sauce and add more cranberry or balsamic to your liking and set aside to cool.

Toss the lettuce leaves, feta and walnuts together.

Lay a bed of salad on a platter, carve the chicken into four pieces and place on the salad. Drizzle the sauce over the top of the chicken and serve immediately.

Roast Chicken with Pineapple Sage Couscous

This is a perfect Monday night recipe. It's super easy, so delicious and you can make a little extra to take to work the next day. I love the combination of fruit with any protein, especially when it's cooked for longer. The natural flavour of the fruit changes from a sharp tang to a deep and hearty sweetness, which pairs with the meat rather than overpowering it. Pineapple is becoming easier and easier to get all year round but it can be pricey — when it is you can just use the canned stuff instead, draining half the juice.

Preparation time: 25 minutes

Cooking time: 1 hour 20 minutes

Feeds: 4

4 cups diced fresh or canned pineapple (reserve 2 tablespoons juice)

2 medium-sized kumara, peeled and diced

1 medium-sized brown onion, diced

1 whole chicken

4 tablespoons olive oil

salt and pepper

big handful of fresh sage leaves, finely sliced

2 cups Israeli couscous

4 cups chicken stock

½ cup pine nuts

Preheat the oven to 240°C.

Toss the pineapple, kumara and onion in a large oven tray along with the juice of the pineapple. Coat the whole chicken well with the olive oil, season generously with salt and pepper and sit it on top of the pineapple mix. Sprinkle over the sage. Put the chicken in the oven and immediately turn the temperature down to 200°C. Roast for 1 hour and 20 minutes, basting with the pan juices every half hour. Before removing from the oven, skewer the thickest part of the chicken to make sure the juices run clear and not pink. If they're still pink the chicken's not cooked, so you'll need to leave it in the oven for longer.

When the chicken is cooked, remove it and the kumara from the pan and rest under tin foil while you make the couscous.

Pour the couscous into a large, heavy-based frying pan over a medium-high heat and toast for 2 minutes or until fragrant. Add the chicken stock, reduce the heat to medium-low, and simmer, stirring regularly, until all the stock has been absorbed (10–15 minutes). Once cooked place the couscous in a large serving bowl.

Pour the roasted pineapple and reserved cooking juices into the pan the couscous was cooked in, bring to a simmer and reduce all the liquid (roughly 3–4 minutes). Mix into the couscous with the kumara and pine nuts and season with salt and pepper. Serve immediately with the whole chicken.

Chicken Tikka

This is one of my favourite recipes. Chicken tikka is a Punjabi dish that is either eaten with fresh onion rings or with a sauce, when it becomes chicken tikka masala. This chicken tikka is accompanied by my take on onion rings and a yoghurt dipping sauce. Use the masala sauce recipe on page 62 to make one of the best curries you will ever eat – and you will have cooked it.

Cooking time: 30 minutes

Preparation time: 3–25 hours (depending on marinating time)

Feeds: 4

CHICKEN TIKKA

1 thumbnail-sized piece of ginger, roughly sliced

3 cloves garlic, crushed

2 green chillies, roughly sliced

100g butter

1 teaspoon ground cumin

1 tablespoon garam masala

1 tablespoon smoked paprika

juice of 1 lemon

1 teaspoon salt

½ cup plain yoghurt

8 boneless, skinless chicken thighs

canola oil for deep-frying

ONION RINGS

1 cup plain flour

1 cup beer (Kingfisher if you want to stick with the Indian theme)

2 large brown onions, cut into 1cm-thick rings

YOGHURT DIPPING SAUCE

½ cup plain yoghurt

2 tablespoons mint sauce (see page 180)

Place the ginger, garlic and chillies in a small saucepan with the butter. Melt the butter over a low heat until it begins to bubble, then transfer to a large bowl. Stir in the spices, lemon juice, salt and yoghurt to make a marinade. Add the chicken and coat well. Cover with plastic wrap and pop in the fridge for at least 2 hours or up to 24 hours.

Take the chicken out of the fridge and bring up to room temperature.

Heat the barbecue grill to medium.

To make the onion rings, pour 2cm of canola oil into a large saucepan and heat over a medium-high heat to 170°C or just before smoking point.

Place the flour in a bowl and make a well in the centre. Pour the beer into the well and mix to a smooth consistency. Dust the onion rings in a little extra flour, then coat them in the batter. Deep-fry the rings in batches until golden (about 3 minutes). Drain on paper towels and set aside until the chicken is cooked.

Cook the chicken on the barbecue grill for 12 minutes on each side or until the juices run clear. Remove from the grill and rest for 5 minutes under tin foil.

To make the dipping sauce, combine the yoghurt with the mint sauce.

Serve the chicken and onion rings with the dipping sauce.

I love the
connection you
get with nature
when you cook
outdoors.

Chicken Tikka Masala

This is the older cousin of the chicken tikka recipe on page 58. It takes a bit longer and is a little bit more advanced but is worth it. The tomato curry sauce is unreal and will change the way you do tomato-based sauces forever. The slow roasting might seem a little strange but it creates the most aromatic flavours ever. I still like to cook the chicken on the barbecue as this gives it the authentic smokiness that makes a tikka masala so good. However, if it's raining and cold, whacking the chicken in the oven will still be pretty good. Use the flat bread recipe on page 162 to take things up another notch.

Preparation time: 3–25 hours (depending on marinating time)

Cooking time: 1½ hours

Feeds: 4

CHICKEN TIKKA

See recipe on page 58

MASALA SAUCE

1 tablespoon ground coriander

1 teaspoon ground cinnamon

½ teaspoon ground cloves

½ teaspoon ground cardamom

2 tablespoons garam masala

6 tomatoes, cored

2 bay leaves

4 tablespoons olive oil

1 large brown onion, diced

2 cloves garlic, diced

2 tablespoons tomato paste

150ml coconut milk

50ml cream

salt and pepper

RICE

2 cups basmati rice

3½ cups water

flat breads to serve (see page 162)

coriander leaves to serve

Follow the first step in the chicken tikka recipe on page 58, including placing the covered chicken in the fridge for at least 2 hours or up to 24 hours.

Preheat the oven to 150°C.

Combine the ground coriander, cinnamon, cloves, cardamom and garam masala in a bowl. Place the tomatoes in an oven tray with the bay leaves, half the spice mixture and 2 tablespoons of the olive oil. Cover the tray with tin foil and roast the tomatoes for 1 hour until they are soft and falling apart. Transfer to a food processor and blend to a purée.

Put the remaining olive oil in a large saucepan on a medium heat, then add the onion and garlic. Cook until translucent and fragrant (about 8 minutes), then add the rest of the spice mixture and stir well. Continue to cook until fragrant (about 5 minutes) before adding the roasted tomato purée, tomato paste, coconut milk and cream. Bring to a simmer, cover with a lid and simmer for a further 25 minutes, stirring every 5 minutes or so. Season with salt and pepper.

Heat the barbecue grill to medium.

Rinse the rice in water until the water runs clear, then combine with the water in a saucepan. Place the lid on and bring to the boil over high heat, then turn the heat down to low and cook for 10 minutes. Remove from the heat and let the rice cool, with the lid on, for a further 5 minutes.

Place the chicken on the barbecue grill and cook for 12 minutes on each side or until the juices run clear. Remove from the grill and rest the chicken under tin foil for 5 minutes before cutting the thighs in half.

Toss the chicken in the curry sauce, giving it one final season with salt and pepper, and serve immediately with the rice and flat bread. Sprinkle with coriander leaves.

Pesto-stuffed Chicken Breast with Balsamic Pasta Salad

While I was writing this book I got chatting to some friends about all our homemade specialties; mine usually come from anything I've gathered myself.

My friends mean a lot to me and I think that's one of the reasons why I love good food. It gives you an excuse to meet up, get off the cell phones, turn off the telly, spin a few yarns. They say families who eat together stay together and I think that's true of friends as well. This wee recipe was a spark from that conversation but is written from memories of dinners past, over which I've made some pretty solid friendships.

Preparation time: 30 minutes

Cooking time: 40 minutes

Feeds: 4

4 boneless, skinless chicken breasts

½ cup basil pesto (see page 176)

juice of 1 lemon

salt and pepper

50g butter

½ cup balsamic vinegar

2 tablespoons honey

pasta dough (see page 154) or 2 cups of your favourite pasta (uncooked)

2 tablespoons olive oil

200g cherry tomatoes, halved

200g feta, crumbled

fresh basil leaves to garnish

Preheat the oven to 200°C.

Place the chicken on a chopping board. With a sharp knife, cut a deep pocket into the side of each breast (be careful not to cut through to the other side). Combine the pesto and lemon juice, then place the stuffing into the pockets you've just cut. Season the chicken with salt and pepper. Place in an oven tray, dot with the butter and cover with baking paper. Roast until the chicken juices run clear (35–40 minutes), removing the baking paper for the last 10–15 minutes to allow some caramelisation on the top of the chicken. Rest the chicken for 10 minutes under tin foil before serving.

Combine the balsamic vinegar and honey in a small saucepan and place over a high heat. Bring to the boil, then turn the heat to low and simmer for 10 minutes. Remove the reduction from the heat and allow to cool.

Bring a saucepan of salted water to a rolling boil. If you're making your own pasta roll it out to the second thinnest setting on the pasta machine and cut into 0.5cm strips. Cook the pasta for 4 minutes or until al dente. Drain, then toss through the olive oil.

Combine the pasta with the cherry tomatoes, feta and balsamic reduction and mix well. Place on a serving platter and top with the chicken breasts, basil leaves and a good grind of pepper.

Buffalo Wings with Ranch Dressing

Preparation time: 20 minutes

Cooking time: 35 minutes

Feeds: 4

BUFFALO SAUCE

3 cloves garlic, minced

½ cup tomato sauce

¼ cup water

¼ cup honey

¼ cup white wine vinegar

2 tablespoons brown sugar

1 tablespoon Dijon mustard

1 tablespoon Worcestershire
sauce

1 tablespoon soy sauce

2 teaspoons onion powder

salt and pepper

1–2 tablespoons hot sauce

WINGS

1kg chicken wings

1 tablespoon salt

2 teaspoons ground black pepper

1 teaspoon ground red pepper

1 teaspoon onion powder

1 cup plain flour

canola oil for deep-frying

handful of celery leaves,
roughly chopped

ranch dressing (see page 178)
to serve

These wings are built for game days or movie nights. I always get excited when good wings are getting passed around, especially when they are followed by ranch dressing. The combination of spicy and creamy, the anticipation of licking your fingers when you've finished eating and the satisfaction of a bone absolutely cleaned of meat — sometimes it's the simple things in life.

To make the buffalo sauce, place the garlic, tomato sauce, water, honey, vinegar, brown sugar, Dijon mustard, Worcestershire and soy sauces, onion powder, and salt and pepper in a saucepan. Bring to the boil over a medium-high heat, then reduce to a simmer for 15–20 minutes. Check the balance of flavours and add hot sauce to taste.

Season the chicken wings with the salt, peppers and onion powder. Place the flour in a bowl and dredge the wings, shaking off the excess.

Pour 3cm of canola oil into a large saucepan or wok and heat it to 170°C or just before smoking point. Fry the chicken, in batches, for 3–4 minutes each side. Drain the chicken on a wire rack over paper towels.

Toss the wings in the buffalo sauce. Scatter over the celery leaves and serve immediately with the ranch dressing for dipping.

A meal begins
with the planting
of a seed.

Chicken Tacos with Refried Beans and Corn Salsa

Preparation time: 20 minutes

Cooking time: 30 minutes plus marinating time

Feeds: 4

CHICKEN

1 tablespoon ground coriander

1 red chilli, finely diced

1 teaspoon paprika

600g chicken tenderloins

REFRIED BEANS

2 x 400g cans black beans

4 cups chicken stock

2 cups water

½ large brown onion, finely diced

2 tablespoons olive oil

salt and pepper

CORN SALSA

2 tablespoons olive oil

½ brown onion, finely diced

2 corn cobs

handful of fresh coriander leaves, finely chopped

1 red chilli, finely chopped

salt and pepper

TO ASSEMBLE

12 soft tacos (see page 174 or storebought)

juice of 3 limes to serve

sour cream to serve

hot sauce to serve

coriander leaves to serve

Although I was born in New Zealand, I lived in America till the age of four. We ate a lot of Mexican food over there and Mum and Dad brought that back with us. Growing up, I remember a lot of taco, nacho and enchilada nights. I feel like I could eat Mexican every day for the rest of my life and not feel disappointed. A fresh corn salsa, refried beans and spicy chicken all under the same roof? Sounds like a good time to me.

Combine the ground coriander, chilli and paprika in a mortar and pestle and bash to a paste. Combine with the chicken and leave to marinate for at least 1 hour.

In a small saucepan, combine the beans, chicken stock and water. Bring to a simmer over a medium-high heat, cover with a lid and cook for about 30 minutes or until soft. Drain the beans, place in a food processor and process to a paste.

Place the onion in a large frying pan with the olive oil and lightly caramelise over a medium-high heat. Add the bean purée and fry lightly. Remove the beans from the pan, season with salt and pepper, and set aside.

For the corn salsa, add the olive oil and onion to a saucepan and cook for 2 minutes until soft. Slice the kernels off the corn cobs and add to the pan. Cook, stirring occasionally, for 5–6 minutes. Remove from the pan, stir through the coriander and chilli, season with salt and pepper, and set the salsa aside.

To cook the chicken, heat a frying pan over medium-high heat with a little olive oil. Cook the chicken in batches for 2–3 minutes each side. Rest on a plate under tin foil to keep warm.

Warm the tacos in a dry frying pan if they're not freshly cooked. Layer up each taco with beans, corn salsa, chicken, a squeeze of lime juice, a dollop of sour cream, a generous pour of hot sauce and some coriander leaves. Dig in.

Jerk Chicken with Jamaican Rice and Peas

Preparation time: 20 minutes

Cooking time: 40 minutes

Feeds: 4

JERK RUB

5 bay leaves

1½ tablespoons dried thyme

2 teaspoons dried rosemary

2 teaspoons ground allspice

2 teaspoons ground ginger

1 teaspoon salt

2 teaspoons onion powder

1 teaspoon black pepper

1½ teaspoons ground cinnamon

1 teaspoon garlic powder

pinch of nutmeg

pinch of paprika

1 teaspoon chilli powder

2 tablespoons sugar

CHICKEN

1kg chicken drumsticks

juice of 1 lime

¼ cup olive oil

RICE AND PEAS

2 tablespoons vegetable oil

½ large brown onion, finely diced

4 cloves garlic, minced

2 cups rice

1 teaspoon salt

1 cup water

1 cup chicken stock

2 cups coconut milk

400g can red kidney beans, drained and rinsed

1 whole red chilli

1 tablespoon dried thyme

lime wedges and coriander to serve

Nope, that's not a typo — for some reason the Jamaicans call the beans in this recipe peas. Regardless of that confusion, they sure know how to cook great food and I've tried to keep this one pretty traditional. Jerk chicken is about as Jamaican as Bob Marley, and rice and peas is the obvious side of choice. On a summer evening, sit out on the sand dunes, munch down a bowl of this and let the beauty of nature sink in.

Note: If you can't find dried thyme or rosemary, just bash some fresh stuff up in a mortar and pestle and use that. Cooking the chicken on a rack will make the skin crispier and help with even cooking.

Preheat the oven to 220°C.

Grind the bay leaves in a mortar and pestle. Combine with the dried thyme and rosemary and mix well. Add the allspice, ginger, salt, onion powder, pepper, cinnamon, garlic powder, nutmeg, paprika, chilli powder and sugar, and mix well. Place in a bowl.

Combine the chicken drumsticks with the lime juice and olive oil and mix well. Drag the chicken through the jerk mixture, making sure the chicken is well coated. Place the drumsticks on a rack sitting in an oven tray. Roast for 35 minutes or until the juices run clear. Rest on a plate under tin foil for 10 minutes.

For the rice and peas, heat the oil in a large saucepan over a medium-high heat and cook the onion until caramelised (roughly 5–6 minutes). Add the garlic and rice and cook for 2–3 minutes. Then add the salt, water, chicken stock, coconut milk, kidney beans, chilli and dried thyme. Bring to a simmer, cover with a lid and continue simmering for 20 minutes. Remove from the heat and let the rice sit for 10 minutes.

Place the chicken on a bed of rice and peas, squeeze some fresh lime juice over the top and sprinkle with coriander.

Chicken Meatballs with Chinese Noodle Soup

It's taken me a while but I'm warming to Chinese cuisine — being a huge fan of noodles has admittedly helped. Noodle soups were the first thing I jumped on when trying out Chinese food and now I find it tough to go past them in a food court. This one has a punchy mushroom-flavoured soup with fresh greens and delish chicken meatballs. Go on, give it a go and get slurping.

Preparation time: 30 minutes

Cooking time: 30 minutes

Feeds: 4

CHICKEN MEATBALLS

1 large brown onion, roughly chopped

1 clove garlic, roughly chopped

1 thumbnail-sized piece of ginger, roughly chopped

2 red chillies, roughly chopped

handful of fresh coriander leaves, roughly chopped

4 teaspoons milk

¾ cup breadcrumbs

600g chicken mince

NOODLE SOUP

1.5 litres chicken stock

¼ cup dried porcini or shiitake mushrooms

2 tablespoons sesame oil

4 tablespoons soy sauce

2 tablespoons rice wine vinegar

1 thumbnail-sized piece of ginger, finely sliced

bunch of bok choi, trimmed

400g hokkien noodles

sliced chillies and chopped spring onions to serve

coriander leaves to serve

Place the onion, garlic, ginger, chillies and coriander leaves in a food processor and whiz until finely chopped.

Combine the milk and breadcrumbs in a separate bowl and leave to soak for a couple of minutes.

Combine the onion mixture with the soaked breadcrumbs and chicken mince, and mix thoroughly. Roll the mixture into little balls.

Heat a heavy-based frying pan with a little oil and cook the meatballs in batches, until well browned all over and cooked through (about 3 minutes each side). Set aside.

For the soup, combine the chicken stock, porcini or shiitake mushrooms, sesame oil, soy sauce, rice wine vinegar and ginger in a large saucepan or wok. Simmer, covered with a lid, for 20 minutes. Add the bok choi leaves and noodles, and simmer for a further 4 minutes, or until the bok choi is al dente.

Combine the chicken meatballs with the noodle soup and add the sliced chillies and spring onion. Divvy up into separate bowls, scatter with coriander leaves and serve immediately.

game

Dry Red Duck Curry

Preparation time: 30 minutes

Cooking time: 30 minutes

Feeds: 4

CURRY PASTE

1 shallot, finely sliced

1 lemongrass stalk, finely sliced

3–4 red chillies, finely sliced (or more, depending on your tolerance)

3 cloves garlic, finely sliced

1 thumbnail-sized piece of ginger, finely sliced

2 tablespoons tomato paste

1 teaspoon ground cumin

1½ teaspoons ground coriander

½ teaspoon ground cinnamon

2 tablespoons fish sauce

1 teaspoon shrimp paste

1 teaspoon caster sugar

juice of 1 lime

2 tablespoons coconut milk

RED DUCK CURRY

600g duck breast (approximately 3 breasts)

100g Brussels sprouts, leaves separated

100g fresh lychees (or drained canned ones)

100g mung bean sprouts

2 spring onions, finely sliced

handful of fresh coriander leaves

lime wedges to serve

When it comes to curries, this would have to be well up there with my favourites. Duck is so rich, but in classic Thai style you also get the sweet, sour and spice. It wouldn't be my cookbook though without a little Kiwi classic in there and that's the Brussels sprouts. You don't necessarily have to serve rice with this curry, although if you're feeding a few I would pop some on. I know lychees aren't traditional but I prefer them because they have a slightly different sweetness to a more traditional fruit like pineapple. The lychees can be swapped out with pineapple, though; fresh is obviously better but canned will also do the trick.

Place the shallot, lemongrass, 1–2 chillies, garlic and ginger in a food processor with the tomato paste, spices, fish sauce, shrimp paste, sugar, lime juice and coconut milk. Blitz on high speed for 2 minutes until well mixed. Season well with salt and pepper and process again for 1 minute.

Score the skin of the duck breast and place skin side down in a cold saucepan. Put the pan over a medium heat and cook the duck skin until crisp and all the fat has rendered out (about 7 minutes). Remove the duck from the pan and rest on a plate, leaving the fat in the pan.

Add the curry paste to the pan and cook until fragrant and the oil rises to the top (7–8 minutes). Toss in the Brussels sprout leaves and lychees.

Cut the duck breasts into strips before returning them to the pan. Cook until the sprout leaves have wilted slightly, then remove the pan from the heat.

Serve the curry in bowls, top with the mung bean sprouts, spring onion, remaining chillies and coriander. Squeeze over lime juice and serve immediately.

Duck, Fig and Hoisin Pizza

This beauty is possibly my favourite pizza – I will always order a duck pizza if possible when I'm out. Pre-cooked confit duck legs are available from good supermarkets and make this dish a whole lot quicker. For all you hunters out there, feel free to use thin slices of wild duck breast instead. Cooking the thinly sliced meat quickly in the oven means it doesn't have time to dry out.

Preparation time: 50 minutes

Cooking time: 8–10 minutes

Makes: 4 medium-sized pizzas

1 batch pizza dough (see page 152)

2 tablespoons soy sauce

2 teaspoons hoisin sauce

1 tablespoon rice wine vinegar

2 teaspoons honey

pinch of 5-spice

pinch of salt

2 confit duck legs, shredded

100g buffalo mozzarella, torn

4 dried figs, roughly chopped

olive oil to drizzle

small bunch of rocket

salt and black pepper

Prepare the pizza dough following the instructions on page 152.

Preheat the oven to 190°C.

Combine the soy and hoisin sauces, rice wine vinegar, honey, 5-spice and salt in a small saucepan over a medium heat. Bring to the boil and reduce till sticky (about 4 minutes). Spread half of the sauce over the pizza dough. Top with shredded duck meat, mozzarella and dried figs, then drizzle with the remaining sauce.

Pop the pizza on a baking tray and cook in the oven until the base is crispy on the bottom (7–10 minutes). Remove from the oven, allow the pizza to cool for a couple of minutes, then drizzle with a little olive oil and toss the rocket on top. Season with salt and pepper, then slice and dig in.

Venison Steaks with Beet and Pecan Salad and Port Sauce

Venison steaks are becoming easier and easier to get hold of in supermarkets and are an incredibly healthy alternative to beef steaks. To the hunters out there, I imagine you might be getting sick of plain old steaks and mash so I thought I'd give you a bit of a fresher option. The silverbeet and beetroot salad is awesome with venison, and with the sweet port sauce you'll never go back to the old way of having veni steaks again.

Preparation time: 30 minutes

Cooking time: 45 minutes

Feeds: 4

500g beetroot, peeled and cut into 1cm cubes

salt and pepper

4 tablespoons olive oil

4 x 200g venison steaks

200g silverbeet leaves, sliced

200g feta, crumbled

1 cup pecans, roughly chopped

juice of 1 orange

1 tablespoon honey

PORT SAUCE

zest of 1 orange

350g jar redcurrant jelly

4 tablespoons port

1 cinnamon stick

salt and pepper

Preheat the oven to 190°C.

Place the beetroot in an oven tray, season with salt and pepper and drizzle with 2 tablespoons of the olive oil. Roast for 45 minutes, tossing every 15 minutes. Remove from the oven and allow to cool.

To make the sauce, place the orange zest, jelly, port and cinnamon in a saucepan over a medium heat and cook until the jelly has melted. Season with salt and pepper and keep the sauce warm.

Coat the venison steaks in 1 tablespoon of the olive oil, then season with salt and pepper. Heat a frying pan to medium-high heat and cook the venison steaks to rare (2–3 minutes each side) or medium-rare (3–4 minutes each side). Remove from the pan and rest on a plate under tin foil for 5 minutes.

Combine the silverbeet, feta and pecans with the beetroot in a bowl and toss well. Whisk the orange juice, remaining olive oil and honey together. Dress the salad.

Divvy out the steaks with a side of heaped salad. Top the steaks with some port sauce and get stuck in.

Roast Venison Loin with Polenta and Mushrooms

Venison, creamy polenta, mushrooms and balsamic? Yes please, every day of the week! I fell in love with cooking after shooting my first deer, so any venison recipe is pretty close to my heart. This one shows off venison's ability to stand up to some pretty heavy flavours. It's not a light meal; you'll feel like you've eaten for the week, but relaxing in the armchair with a glass of red afterwards will be heavenly. Be careful not to overcook the venison, which due to its low fat content can happen very quickly — watch it carefully and allow it to rest properly. If you need a hit of greens, a wee side salad of rocket with an extra drizzle of balsamic would hit the spot.

Preparation time: 20 minutes

Cooking time: 40 minutes

Feeds: 4

POLENTA

2 cups milk

1½ cups water

½ teaspoon salt

¾ cup polenta

2 tablespoons butter

¼ cup grated Parmesan

MUSHROOMS

400g field mushrooms, stalks trimmed

2 tablespoons olive oil

1 tablespoon balsamic vinegar

2 cloves garlic, minced

salt and pepper

VENISON

800g venison loin

olive oil for cooking

salt and pepper

Place the milk, water and salt in a medium-sized saucepan and bring to a simmer over a medium-high heat. Slowly pour in the polenta and whisk to combine. Reduce the heat to low and partially cover with the lid. Cook for about 30 minutes, whisking vigorously every 5 minutes. Once the polenta is cooked, stir in the butter and grated Parmesan, check the seasoning, cover and keep warm.

Preheat the oven to 180°C.

Wash any dirt off the mushrooms and place in an oven tray. Drizzle with the olive oil and balsamic vinegar and toss in the garlic. Season well with salt and pepper. Roast in the oven for 20 minutes, then keep warm.

Coat the venison in a liberal amount of olive oil and season well with salt and pepper. Place in a hot ovenproof pan and brown well on the stove top on all sides. Finish cooking the venison in the oven for 8 minutes. Remove from the oven and rest the meat under tin foil for 10 minutes before slicing.

Place a generous spoonful of polenta on each plate, along with some sliced venison loin. Top with mushrooms and drizzle with balsamic vinegar.

lamb

Lamb Neck Pappardelle

Lamb neck sounds hideous but it's a beautiful cut of meat. It takes time to cook but the results are more than worth it. The process of thickening the liquid here may seem a little fiddly but it adds bucketloads of flavour. Don't be scared of the anchovies either – they add a depth of saltiness to the dish but definitely don't leave it tasting fishy.

Note: Fresh pasta makes a huge difference and takes this dish from a 10 out of 10 to out of this world. See page 154 for my homemade pasta recipe.

Preparation time: 25 minutes

Cooking time: 2 hours

Feeds: 4–5

LAMB NECK

1kg lamb neck

2 tablespoons olive oil

salt and pepper

1 large brown onion, roughly diced

4 cloves garlic

1 large carrot, peeled and roughly diced

1 celery stalk, roughly diced

50g anchovies

3 cups good-quality beef stock

1 cup good-quality red wine

small handful of fresh thyme sprigs

small handful of fresh rosemary stalks

PAPPARDELLE

pasta dough (see page 154) or 350g storebought fettuccini

1 tablespoon olive oil

1 teaspoon flaky sea salt

100g Parmesan, shaved

fresh flat-leaf parsley to serve

Preheat the oven to 150°C.

Take a large casserole dish and warm it over a low temperature on the stove top. Coat the lamb neck in olive oil and then season liberally with salt and pepper. Turn up the heat to medium-high and, in batches if required, brown the lamb neck all over. Remove the lamb from the dish and turn the heat down to low.

Toss the onion, garlic, carrot and celery in the casserole dish and cook until the onion begins to turn opaque (about 7 minutes). Add the anchovies and cook until fragrant (about 2 minutes).

Add all the remaining lamb neck ingredients to the dish, increase the temperature to high and bring to a simmer. Return the lamb to the dish, place the lid on top and cook in the oven for 1½ hours until the meat is tender and pulls away easily from the bone.

Strain the liquid from the dish into a large saucepan over a medium-high heat and reduce down by three-quarters or until syrupy (about 20 minutes). Meanwhile, shred the lamb from the bones and discard the bones from the dish. Return the liquid to the lamb and place back in the oven (turned off) until the pasta is cooked.

Bring a saucepan of salted water to a rolling boil. If you're making your own pasta, roll the pasta out to the second thinnest setting on the pasta machine. Roll the sheets of pasta into a tube and cut into slices approximately 0.5cm wide (it will swell when cooked). Place the pasta into the water and cook for 4 minutes (or according to packet instructions) until al dente. Drain the pasta, and toss in the oil and salt.

Serve the pappardelle and lamb immediately, top with a generous amount of shaved parmesan and flat-leaf parsley.

Lamb Andhra Curry

2 cups basmati rice

3½ cups water

handful of fresh coriander leaves, roughly torn

flat bread (see page 162) to serve

Preparation time: 1–24 hours (depending on marinating time)

Cooking time: 1 hour

Feeds: 4

SPICE MIX

2 tablespoons white poppy seeds

2 teaspoons ground cloves

2 teaspoons ground cinnamon

2 teaspoons black peppercorns

2 teaspoons salt

8 teaspoons fennel seeds

5 dried chillies

10 cloves garlic, finely chopped

100g ginger, finely chopped

CURRY

juice of 2 large lemons

700g lamb shoulder (deboned), cut into large cubes

2 brown onions, finely sliced

2 teaspoons turmeric

1–3 teaspoons chilli powder (to taste – I go the full three but I like it hot)

5 tablespoons grapeseed oil

400g can tomatoes

10 curry leaves

2½ cups lamb (or beef) stock

1½ cups cream

I love having a curry night, with a few people bringing their best renditions from India, Sri Lanka or Thailand. I've always leaned towards chicken curries, usually from India, but it all changed with this spicy number. The depth of flavour from the massive amount of ginger and garlic goes so well with the lamb.

Note: I love a good flat bread to dip in my curry. Check out my recipe on page 162. It's super simple and quick and will take your curry night to the next level.

Grind the poppy seeds, cloves, cinnamon, peppercorns, salt, fennel seeds and chilli to a fine dust in a mortar and pestle. And the garlic and ginger and grind to a paste.

Add a third of the spice mix to the lemon juice. Rub into the lamb pieces and leave for at least 1 hour or up to a day to marinate.

Place the onions in a large saucepan with the remaining spice mix, the turmeric, chilli powder and grapeseed oil. Cook over a medium heat until the mixture is fragrant and almost dry (about 7 minutes). Add the marinated lamb and brown well on all sides. Add the canned tomatoes and curry leaves as well as 2 cups of the lamb stock. Cook until the fat from the lamb is visible on the side of the pan, and almost dry. Add the cream and remaining lamb stock and cook until the lamb is tender (30–40 minutes). Check the seasoning, adding more salt if required. Leave the pan on the heat but turn it right down while you cook the rice.

Rinse the rice in water until the water runs clear, then combine with the water in a saucepan. Cover with the lid and bring to the boil over high heat, then turn the heat down to low and cook for 10 minutes. Remove from the heat and let the rice cool, with the lid on, for a further 5 minutes.

Top some rice with a healthy spoonful of curry and more of the sauce. Finish with some coriander and serve immediately with flat breads.

Lamb Rack with Baby Potatoes and Dijonnaise

Preparation time: 30 minutes

Cooking time: 20 minutes

Feeds: 4

500g baby potatoes, scrubbed

2 tablespoons salt

50g butter

2 x lamb racks (Frenched)

2 tablespoons olive oil

salt and pepper

1 cup Tim's mayo (see page 150)

4 tablespoons Dijon mustard

handful of fresh mint leaves, roughly chopped

I doubt it gets more Kiwi than a rack of lamb with some beautiful baby potatoes. Add the flavours of mint and mustard and you'll be greasing up to Grandma so much she'll just give you that weird antique vase you've always wanted. Although you can cook a lamb rack purely on the stove top, I love the taste and texture it gets when you caramelise it first then whack it in the oven. If you want some more veges, a crisp lettuce salad with a drizzle of the Dijonnaise would be yum.

Note: If you don't have an ovenproof saucepan (rubber handles don't like ovens) a small oven tray on your stove top or the barbecue with all the dials cranked up can work just as well.

Preheat the oven to 220°C.

Place the potatoes in a large saucepan, cover with cold water, add the salt and bring to the boil over a high heat. Cook until the potatoes can be pierced with a fork but don't crumble apart (6–8 minutes, depending on their size). Drain and return to the pan. Add the butter and place the lid on top. Leave until you are ready to serve.

Rub the lamb racks with the olive oil and season well with salt and pepper. Heat an ovenproof frying pan over a medium-high heat until sizzling hot (test by adding a drop of oil). Add the lamb and brown well on all sides, then throw the pan in the oven for 8 minutes for medium-rare (or 7 minutes for rare and 10 for medium). Remove the lamb from the pan and rest on a chopping board under tin foil for the same amount of time it was in the oven.

Combine the mayo and mustard, then taste and adjust the flavours to your liking.

Toss the mint leaves with the potatoes, and season with salt and pepper.

Cut the lamb racks in half and place a big dollop of the Dijonnaise on top. Give each plate a generous spoonful of the beautiful baby potatoes and serve immediately.

Lamb Loin with Roast Pumpkin and Spiced Labneh

Preparation time: 30 minutes

Cooking time: 40 minutes

Feeds: 4

1kg butternut pumpkin, peeled and cut into thick wedges

50g butter

salt and pepper

800g lamb loin (deboned)

3 tablespoons olive oil

3 tablespoons honey

1 teaspoon ground coriander

1 teaspoon ground cumin

1 teaspoon ground caraway

1 teaspoon cayenne pepper

1 teaspoon chilli flakes

2 cloves garlic, minced

1 cup labneh

juice of 1 lemon

small bunch of fresh mint leaves, finely sliced

pumpkin seeds to serve

torn mint leaves to serve

I love how versatile lamb is, but in New Zealand I think we tend to play it with a pretty straight bat. This recipe is designed to encourage you to experiment with some beautiful Middle Eastern ingredients, which go so well with lamb and are becoming readily available on our shores. Labneh is a cheese made from yoghurt; ricotta is a good substitute, but labneh is much creamier. Serving the lamb with spiced labneh and roast pumpkin is a subtle way of getting Uncle Barry the dairy farmer to branch out a little.

Preheat the oven to 200°C.

Place the pumpkin in an oven tray, dot the butter over the wedges and season generously with salt and pepper. Roast in the oven for 40 minutes, turning once.

Coat the lamb loin in 2 tablespoons of the olive oil and season with salt and pepper. Heat an ovenproof frying pan over a medium-high heat. Brown the lamb on all sides then pop it in the oven for 6 minutes. Take the lamb out of the oven and brush all over with the honey then allow to rest under tin foil for 10 minutes.

Toast the spices in a dry frying pan over a high heat until fragrant. Add the remaining olive oil and the garlic and cook again until fragrant. Tip the spice mix into a bowl and allow to cool. When cool, add the labneh, lemon juice and mint. Mix well and season with salt and pepper.

Toast the pumpkin seeds in a dry frying pan over a high heat for 3 minutes.

Chuck a few pumpkin slices on each plate. Slice the lamb and divvy up. Dollop some spiced labneh on top and sprinkle with the toasted pumpkin seeds and torn mint leaves.

Roast Lamb with Celeriac Remoulade and Mint Sauce

Don't be put off by the big French word in the title. It's a dish of mayo and raw celeriac — incredibly easy to make, and delicious. Celeriac is quickly becoming my favourite root vegetable because of its subtle, fresh flavour combined with the texture of a hearty carb that's going to fill you up. The rest of this dish is a Kiwi classic really: mint sauce and roast lamb. Switch on the All Blacks and tuck into a good old-fashioned roast with a bit of French flair — not on the rugby field though.

Preheat the oven to 180°C.

Combine the butter, garlic and salt and pepper. Make small slices in the lamb leg a couple of centimetres apart and massage the butter into the lamb. Place the lamb in an oven tray and roast for 25 minutes per 500g of meat for medium-rare (or 30 minutes for medium). Baste the lamb every 20 minutes. Remove from the oven and rest the lamb under tin foil for 10 minutes.

Combine the lemon juice, mayo, mint and olive oil, and season with salt and pepper. Peel and grate the celeriac as quickly as possible then toss in the minted mayo — celeriac oxidises (turns brown) quickly once peeled and grated unless you put it in some acid. Feel free to do this in batches and stir it into the mayo as you go.

Divide the celeriac remoulade between serving plates. Top with freshly carved lamb and a drizzle of mint sauce.

Preparation time: 30 minutes

Cooking time: 1 hour 40 minutes (depending on size of lamb leg)

Feeds: 4

ROAST LAMB

100g butter (softened in the microwave for 10 seconds)

5 cloves garlic, minced

2 tablespoons salt

1 tablespoon pepper

1 lamb leg roast (bone in)

CELERIAC REMOULADE

juice of 2 lemons

½ cup Tim's mayo (see page 150)

handful of fresh mint leaves, finely chopped

2 tablespoons olive oil

salt and pepper

1 large celeriac

mint sauce (see page 180) to serve

seafood

Poached Crayfish Sandwich with Malt Mayo Slaw

This is my favourite way to eat crayfish — straight from the sea. Pop it in a pot and, in the time it cooks, the mayo can be made. Slap the tail in some fresh white bread with a good smear of mayo: YUM. If I have the patience to make it home I'll add some cabbage for fresh crunch, as well as the coriander and sesame seeds. It would be rude not to have a beer with this one.

Note: To humanely cook the crayfish I either pop it in the freezer for half an hour or sit it in fresh water for the same time. When I go on a dive, I make sure I take at least 1.5 litres of fresh water with me so I can do this. It may sound like a long time but, by the time you've cleaned and rinsed your gear, it'll be ready to cook.

Preparation time: 20 minutes

Cooking time: 10 minutes

Feeds: 4

2 crayfish

2–3 litres salted water

1 cup Tim's mayo (see page 150)

3 tablespoons malt vinegar

2 tablespoons sesame seeds

¼ cabbage, very finely sliced

salt and pepper

a loaf of fresh white bread

butter for spreading

handful of fresh coriander leaves

Bring enough salted water to completely cover the crayfish to a rolling boil (you can cook the crayfish one at a time if you have to). Cook for 7 minutes if a smaller cray or up to 9 minutes for the big boys. Remove from the water to rest and finish cooking.

While the cray is cooking, make the mayo and add the malt vinegar to taste. Crayfish meat is very sweet so don't worry if it tastes a little tart.

Toast the sesame seeds in a dry frying pan over a high heat. Toss the sesame seeds through the cabbage along with half of the mayo. Season well with salt and pepper.

Remove the flesh from the crayfish tail by cutting the tail in half lengthways and prying it from the shell. Keep the legs for crunching through later. Butter a slice of bread, add a generous amount of the slaw, half a crayfish tail, drizzle with some more mayo, top with coriander and get stuck in.

Crispy Salmon with Middle Eastern Parsnip Chips and Mint Pistachio Pesto

Preparation time: 20 minutes

Cooking time: 35 minutes

Feeds: 4

PARSNIP CHIPS

6 parsnips, peeled and cut into fries

2 tablespoons olive oil

1 teaspoon ground allspice

1 teaspoon ground cumin

½ teaspoon ground cinnamon

1 teaspoon salt

½ teaspoon black pepper

MINT PISTACHIO PESTO

½ cup fresh mint leaves

¼ cup fresh flat-leaf parsley leaves

½ cup pistachio nuts

juice of 1 lime

¼ cup olive oil

CRISPY SALMON

800g salmon fillets

salt and pepper

olive oil for coating

½ cup plain Greek yoghurt to serve

1 tablespoon sumac to serve

Salmon is my mum's favourite food, and one Christmas while I was cooking her a massive fillet I made this pesto to go with it. It is super clean and fresh, which balances the richness of the salmon so well. Combine that with the nuttiness of the parsnip and the earthy spices and it becomes a delicious and healthy Middle Eastern take on fish and chips.

Note: Sumac can be found at Indian or Middle Eastern spice shops or more specialist supermarkets. Sumac has an earthy, citrus note, and has quickly become one of my favourite spices for seafood.

Preheat the oven to 190°C.

Toss the parsnip fries with the olive oil and spices in a large oven tray. Roast in the oven for 25 minutes.

Place the mint, parsley, pistachios, lime juice and half the olive oil in a food processor, and blend until well incorporated, adding more oil if required. (Pistachio nuts have very little natural oil so you need quite a bit of olive oil.)

Remove the parsnips from the oven and toss. Increase the oven temperature to 240°C. Return the parsnips to the oven to cook for an additional 5–10 minutes until crispy. Keep a close eye on them to make sure they don't burn.

Lay the salmon out on a chopping board, skin side up, season well with salt and pepper and coat the skin with olive oil. Heat a heavy-based frying pan over a medium-high heat and add the salmon, skin side down, pressing with a spatula so the skin makes contact with the pan and goes nice and crispy. Once the skin is browned and crispy (4–5 minutes), flip the salmon over and cook for a further 3–4 minutes or until cooked through.

Place the salmon skin side up on plates, top with some pesto and a little more salt and pepper. Throw on the parsnip chips, drizzle over some yoghurt and sprinkle with sumac.

Beautiful, fresh
produce doesn't need
a lot done to it.

Creamy Paua on Toast

Preparation time: 10 minutes

Cooking time: 20 minutes

Feeds: 4

2 paua

salt and pepper

50g butter

1 small brown onion, finely sliced

2 cloves garlic, finely sliced

½ chorizo, diced

½ cup good-quality red wine (pinot noir)

¼ cup cream

1 teaspoon smoked paprika

a loaf of good, crusty white bread like ciabatta

This is another one of those recipes that, if you are prepared, you can make at the beach. I'll get everything ready before heading out to a spot where I know I'll get a couple of paua, then it's just a matter of adding them to a hot pan. Don't forget the old knife and fork and a couple of plates.

Note: There are a couple of ways to tenderise paua. Most people remove it from the shell then bash it with a stone until it 'relaxes'. Some good friends of mine boil their paua for 2 minutes in the shell, then let them sit for 10 minutes. Not only does this make shelling them a LOT easier but it also seems to relax the foot quite well. You choose though.

Remove the paua foot from the shell and gut (see note above), then slice as thinly as possible. Season with salt and pepper and set aside. Melt half the butter in a frying pan over a medium heat until bubbling. Add the onion and garlic, and cook until translucent and fragrant (about 7 minutes). Add the chorizo and cook for about 3–4 minutes until it begins to brown. Transfer the mixture to a bowl and set aside. Add the paua to the same pan and sear until lightly browned (about 5 minutes).

Add the red wine and reduce by half. Return the chorizo mixture to the pan along with the cream and smoked paprika and reduce by half again. Remove from the heat.

Add the remaining butter to the pan and let the paua sit in the creamy sauce for 5 minutes without stirring. Meanwhile, cut and toast some slices of bread. Stir the creamy paua and season to taste with salt and pepper. Serve immediately on toast.

Seafood Spaghetti with Bacon, Leek and Caramelised Fennel

I usually make this with pipi but cockles or tuatua work well too. Pipi are beautifully sweet and salty with the ability to stand up to some pretty bold flavours, but for some reason are so underrated. I have seen them in some supermarkets, but they can be found at most estuaries around New Zealand, and with a bit of digging you can easily get enough for a dinner or two. (Tuatua can be found at many New Zealand beaches too.) If you are stuck for where to find them, pop into your local fishing store — they should have a good idea of where the pipi are. Take the kids and make a fun family outing of it.

Note: If you are digging your own, soak the pipi in a bucket of fresh water for at least 12 hours to ensure they spit out all the sand.

Preparation time: 25 minutes

Cooking time: 35 minutes

Feeds: 4

1 fennel bulb, trimmed and thinly sliced

50g butter

pinch of salt

4 slices bacon, diced

1 leek, diced

½ cup cream

salt and pepper

pasta dough (see page 154)

500g pipi or cockles

freshly shaved Parmesan to serve

chopped flat-leaf parsley to serve

Place the fennel, butter and salt in a heavy-based frying pan over a medium-high heat and cook for 20 minutes, stirring regularly, until the fennel is well browned and caramelised. Remove the fennel from the pan but don't wash the pan — you'll use it in the next step.

Add the bacon and leek to the same pan the fennel was cooked in. Place over a medium heat and cook for 5–10 minutes, allowing the bacon to crisp up and the leeks to soften. Add the cream and season to taste with salt and pepper. Reduce the heat to low, allowing the cream to thicken slowly.

Bring a large saucepan of salted water to the boil. If you're making your own pasta, remove the dough from the fridge now. Knead the dough on a floured bench for a few minutes, then get your pasta machine ready. Roll the pasta out to the second thinnest setting on the machine. When you have the pasta nice and thin, take it through the setting that cuts it into thin ribbons. Cook the pasta for 4 minutes or until al dente. Drain.

At the same time as putting the pasta on, place the pipi or cockles in with the creamy leeks and bacon and turn up the heat. Add a little more cream if required and bring to a simmer. By the time the pasta is cooked the pipi should be opening and cooked too.

Toss the pasta through the creamy sauce, add the caramelised fennel and give it one last good stir. Season with salt and pepper, top with freshly shaved Parmesan cheese and parsley, and serve immediately.

Prawn, Fennel, Onion and Lemon Pizza

We had a pizza night in the *MasterChef* house one Friday, and this was one of the resulting creations. The dough had been made during the day, and that night when everyone came home we all pitched in and a few different flavour combinations were born. Although many moments of the competition were difficult, being able to come home and spend time with like-minded people and share in good food brought sunshine to my day. Those memories, for me, will last far longer than the ones in the kitchen.

Preparation time: 50 minutes

Cooking time: 8–10 minutes

Makes: 4 medium-sized pizzas

1 batch pizza dough (see page 152)

3 tablespoons tomato paste

100g buffalo mozzarella, torn

200g prawns, shelled and deveined

½ small fennel bulb, sliced (fronds reserved for garnish)

½ small red onion, finely sliced

1 lemon

olive oil to drizzle

salt and pepper

Prepare the pizza dough following the instructions on page 152.

Preheat the oven to 190°C.

Spread the base with tomato paste and top with mozzarella, prawns, fennel slices and red onion. Remove the skin from the lemon and cut into segments. Cut the segments in half and scatter over the pizza.

Pop the pizza on a baking tray and cook in the oven till the base is crispy on the bottom (7–10 minutes). Remove from the oven, allow the pizza to cool for 3 minutes before drizzling with a little olive oil, garnishing with the fennel fronds and seasoning well with salt and pepper.

Ginger Beer Tempura Oyster Sliders with Japanese Slaw

Tempura-battered seafood is tough to beat, as is a good oyster. This recipe combines these two beauties in a Japanese-inspired slider. The tempura batter needs to be made at the last minute and kept really cold. This will make it light and fluffy rather than solid and doughy. I've used ginger beer instead of the traditional soda water in the batter, as it provides a gentle sweetness to counteract the richness of the oyster. If you can't get your hands on oysters, mussels are a good substitute.

Note: For this recipe I like the idea of the bun being more of a hotdog roll as you can slide a few oysters in without them falling out the side. There are instructions for how to shape the rolls in the slider recipe on page 156.

Preparation time: 20 minutes

Cooking time: 20 minutes

Feeds: 4

WASABI MAYO

½ cup Tim's mayo (see page 150)

2½ teaspoons wasabi (to taste)

JAPANESE SLAW

2 large radishes, cut into thin strips

½ Savoy cabbage, finely sliced

2 tablespoons sesame oil

2 tablespoons soy sauce

3 tablespoons sesame seeds

TEMPURA OYSTERS

2 cups canola oil

3 dozen oysters

1 cup cornflour

1 cup plain flour

1 tablespoon baking powder

200ml ice-cold ginger beer

8 slider buns (see page 156) or hotdog rolls (storebought)

Whisk the mayo and wasabi together. Pop in the fridge till required.

Toss the radishes and cabbage in a bowl with the sesame oil and soy sauce. Toast the sesame seeds in a dry frying pan over medium heat until golden and fragrant. Toss through the salad. Check the seasoning and put in the fridge till required.

Heat the canola oil in a wok or deep-fryer to 170°C or just before smoking point. Shuck the oysters and pat them dry with paper towels – this will help the batter to stick.

Combine the flours and baking powder in a large bowl, stirring well. Just before cooking the oysters, add the ginger beer and stir well – the mixture should be thick enough to coat your finger. Dredge 5–6 oysters at a time in the batter and then place in the hot oil and fry till golden brown (about 3 minutes). Remove the oysters from the hot oil and drain on paper towels. Repeat with the remaining oysters.

Cut the buns and smother each side with wasabi mayo. Add 3–4 oysters per bun and top with Japanese slaw. Serve immediately.

Thai Whitebait Salad

Preparation time: 20 minutes

Cooking time: 35 minutes

Feeds: 4

RICE

1½ cups jasmine rice

1 clove garlic, minced

1 thumbnail-sized piece of ginger, minced

1 teaspoon salt

400ml can coconut milk

1 cup water

SYRUP

1 cup water

½ cup caster sugar

2–3 red chillies, finely diced

1 thumbnail-sized piece of ginger, finely diced

SALAD

5 spring onions, finely sliced

2 cups mung bean sprouts

2 red chillies, finely sliced

¼ red cabbage, finely sliced

½ cup peanuts, crushed

¼ cup fresh coriander, finely sliced

zest of 2 limes

WHITEBAIT

2 cups vegetable oil

250g whitebait (the more the merrier though)

½ cup plain flour

salt and pepper

lime wedges and coriander leaves to serve

A few people are going to shoot me for saying this, but I'm not a huge whitebait fritter fan. Eighty per cent of you are going to rubbish this recipe because how can you waste whitebait on a salad? The other 20 per cent though are either not fritter fans either, or are looking for something different to do with whitebait.

Look no further than this bad boy. It's got everything a classic Thai dish should have – heat, sweet, sour and power. The star of the dish though is the good old Kiwi whitebait, fried till crispy with the flavour that we all love.

Rinse the rice well with water until the water runs clear. Mix together the rice, garlic, ginger, salt, coconut milk and water. Cover and bring to the boil, then reduce the heat to low and simmer for 30 minutes. Remove the rice from the heat but keep the lid on till ready to serve.

Place all the syrup ingredients in a small saucepan over a medium-high heat and bring to the boil. Reduce the heat to medium and reduce the liquid by two-thirds (about 5–8 minutes) until all that remains is a sweet and spicy syrup. Remove from the heat and keep warm.

Toss the spring onions, bean sprouts, chillies, cabbage, peanuts, coriander and lime juice in a bowl. Set aside.

Heat the oil in a large wok to 170°C or just before smoking point. Dry the whitebait well on paper towels. Place the flour in a bowl, season with salt and pepper and toss the whitebait through. Fry the whitebait in batches until crispy (about 2 minutes), stirring regularly. Drain the whitebait on paper towels.

Spoon some rice into the bottom of serving bowls, top with the salad, then the whitebait. Drizzle a generous amount of syrup over the top and finish with a squeeze of lime juice and some coriander leaves.

Salt-baked Fish with Green Beans and Tartare Sauce

I first had this dish when I flatted with some good friends who had lived in Europe for a while. Through them I got the opportunity to try a lot of foods I had never even heard of. When I caught a decent snapper out fishing one day, I gave it to my friends as a way of saying thanks – they used it to whip up a salt-baked snapper. At first I thought they were crazy, but then I tasted it and, boy, they were on to something. I love the flavour the salt imparts into the flesh, and with the crisp green beans and a good old tartare sauce it's the perfect way to end a summer day spent on the water. Some crispy roast potatoes would bulk up this meal a little bit.

Preparation time: 20 minutes

Cooking time: 25 minutes

Feeds: 4

1kg coarse rock salt

2 eggs

1½ tablespoons fennel seeds

zest and juice of 2 lemons

1 whole snapper with scales on (or trevally or terakihi)

big handful of fresh flat-leaf parsley

200g green beans

50g butter

2 cloves garlic, minced

salt and pepper

½ cup tartare sauce (see page 170) to serve

Preheat the oven to its highest heat.

Mix the salt, eggs, fennel seeds and zest of 1 lemon together until you have a sticky mixture. Stuff the gut cavity of the fish with half of the parsley. Pour half of the salt mixture into an oven tray and spread it out evenly. Lay the fish on top, then cover the snapper with the remaining salt mixture. Pat down firmly to encase the fish in a thick layer of salt. Bake in the oven for 15 minutes. The fish will be cooked when a knife pierced through the salt and into the middle of the fish feels hot to touch on your lip. Remove from the oven and rest for at least 10 minutes.

Bring a large saucepan of salted water to the boil. Prepare an ice bath to blanch the beans. Cook the beans in the water until they turn bright green (about 2 minutes). Drain, then shock in the iced water to stop them cooking.

Heat a large frying pan over a medium-high heat. Add the butter and garlic and cook until fragrant, then add the beans and juice from both the lemons. Reserve the lemon zest from the second lemon. Cook for a couple of minutes until the beans are hot and coated in lemon butter, then season with salt and pepper and keep warm.

The salt crust on the fish will be rock hard. Break the crust around the edges with the back of a spoon and the whole top will peel off. Place the fish on a serving platter and surround it with the beans and lemon butter. Sprinkle with the remaining lemon zest and parsley, and serve tartare sauce on the side.

desserts & sweets

Aunty Anna's Banana Cake

Preparation time: 20 minutes

Cooking time: 30–40 minutes

Makes: 1 x 23cm cake

125g butter

1 teaspoon vanilla extract

1 cup caster sugar

2 eggs

2 cups self-raising flour

¼ teaspoon baking soda

3 large bananas, mashed (enough for 1 cup mashed bananas)

4 tablespoons sour cream

¼ cup icing sugar to dust

This recipe is pretty close to my heart. Aunty Anna is my uncle's sister-in-law, a gifted cook and baker and one of the most generous people I know. I lived with my uncle for a few years and have been on a fair number of fishing adventures with him. Whenever Aunty Anna's husband came along, he'd bring this cake. We usually leave before dawn so this cake gets brought out about 10am when the first groans of hunger hit. My uncle uses his bait-covered hands to rip off pieces and literally throw them to everyone on the boat. Usually I wouldn't touch such a thing but banana cake's a weakness of mine and this is a good one – even squid remnants can't destroy it. So here's to Aunty Anna and the best banana cake I know.

Aunty Anna usually just dusts the top of the cake with icing sugar but feel free to use any icing you like; chocolate or lemon work really well.

Preheat the oven to 180°C. Grease a 23cm cake tin and line with baking paper.

Place the butter and vanilla in an electric mixer. Mix with the paddle attachment on low speed until combined. Gradually add the sugar and cream the mixture till smooth. Add the eggs one at a time and beat to an even consistency.

Sift the flour and baking soda into a large bowl, then add to the mixer and beat on low speed for a couple of minutes. Take the mashed banana and mix together with the sour cream. Add to the mixer and beat on low speed until well combined.

Pour the batter into the prepared tin and bake for 30–40 minutes (this will depend on the size of your tin and the thickness of the cake), or until a skewer inserted in the centre comes out clean. Remove the cake from the oven and let it cool for 10 minutes.

After 10 minutes, turn the cake out on to a wire rack. Allow to cool for another 20 minutes before dusting with icing sugar and digging in.

Never-fail Chocolate Cake with Chocolate Praline Ganache

My sister gave me this recipe, and topping it with chocolate ganache and macadamia nuts is a master stroke. For me, cake recipes have to be idiot-proof because of my tendency to overlook minor details; I can happily say that each time I've made this one I've looked like a cake boss. So get stuck in and enjoy!

Note: Melted sugar reaches upwards of 160°C so be very careful and don't dip your finger in the praline for a taste!

Preparation time: 2 hours

Cooking time: 1 hour 20 minutes

Makes: 1 large cake

- 2 cups high-grade flour
- 2 teaspoons baking powder
- 2 teaspoons baking soda
- 2 cups caster sugar
- ¾ cup cocoa
- 1 teaspoon salt
- 2 eggs
- 1 cup milk
- 1 cup vegetable oil
- 2 teaspoons vanilla extract
- 1 teaspoon instant coffee
- 1 cup boiling water

CHOCOLATE PRALINE GANACHE

- ¾ cup caster sugar
- 250g milk chocolate
- 800ml double cream
- ¾ cup macadamia nuts

Preheat the oven to 150°C. Grease and line a large cake tin.

Sift the flour, baking powder and baking soda into a large bowl or the bowl of an electric mixer, then add the caster sugar, cocoa and salt and combine.

Add the eggs, milk, oil and vanilla to the dry ingredients. Using a spatula or the mixer's paddle attachment, beat for 2 minutes or until well incorporated.

Combine the coffee and water in a bowl, stir well and add to the batter – it will be very thin but that's okay. Pour the batter into a large cake tin and cook for 1 hour and 20 minutes or until a skewer inserted in the centre comes out clean.

While the cake is cooking, make the ganache. Place the sugar in a wide saucepan over a medium heat. Allow the sugar to melt and caramelise, stirring regularly to ensure even melting, until it's a beautiful caramel colour (about 10 minutes). Pour the mixture on to a piece of baking paper and allow to cool and harden. Once the praline has hardened place it in a food processor and blend to a fine crumb.

Place the chocolate in a large, microwave-proof bowl and melt in 30-second intervals, stirring well in between. When the chocolate has melted and is lump-free, add the praline crumb and stir again. The praline will not melt completely so don't worry if it's a little grainy.

Bring 300ml of the cream to the boil in a small saucepan. Pour roughly one third into the chocolate mixture and stir well until it's a nice even colour. Pour the remaining boiled cream into the chocolate mixture and combine well. Add the chocolate mixture to the remaining cold cream, stirring well, and place in the fridge for 1 hour or until cold.

Remove the cake from the oven and cool in the tin for 10 minutes before turning out to cool completely on a wire rack.

Lightly toast the macadamia nuts in a dry frying pan for 4–5 minutes over a high heat. Allow to cool, then crush the nuts with the palm of your hand. Whip the ganache to medium peaks and spread over the cooled cake. Top with the crushed macadamias and enjoy.

Pumpkin Pie with Cream Cheese and Cream Cream

American cuisine has become pretty popular in New Zealand over the last few years and I'm loving it. It may seem heavy and way over the top but when it comes to a good feed (especially dessert) is that not the way we like it here? This pumpkin pie recipe is exactly that: comfort food that is probably not the best for you but feels like a cosy duvet cuddling you on a cold winter's night. I've added my own little cream to the mix too. I got a lot of stick in the *MasterChef* competition for making a recipe with the word cream in it three times – but I just love the stuff so I thought I would share it here so you can get in on it too.

Preparation time: 40 minutes

Cooking time: 35–45 minutes

Makes 1 x 23cm pie

CRUST

pie crust (see page 166) or
2 sheets frozen shortcrust
pastry, thawed

FILLING

500g pumpkin, peeled and cut into small cubes

3 eggs

½ cup caster sugar

⅓ cup brown sugar

¾ cup double cream

1 teaspoon vanilla extract

1½ teaspoons ground cinnamon

½ teaspoon ground ginger

¼ teaspoon ground cloves

½ teaspoon salt

CREAM CHEESE AND CREAM CREAM

¼ cup cream

150g cream cheese

1 tablespoon caster sugar

¼ teaspoon vanilla extract

Prepare your pie crust following the instructions on page 166.

Roll out the dough to 2cm larger than your pie dish – I use a 23cm dish. Gently press the dough into the dish so that it lines the bottom and sides evenly (try not to pull or stretch the dough). Fold the edges of the dough underneath itself to create a thicker crust that rests on the lip of the dish. Pop the crust in the fridge while you make the filling.

Cook the pumpkin in a large saucepan of boiling water until soft (10–20 minutes, depending on the size of the cubes). Drain, then mash the pumpkin to a smooth purée. Set aside to cool.

Preheat the oven to 220°C.

In a large bowl, or the bowl of an electric mixer, whisk the eggs and both sugars together until smooth. Add 2 cups of the pumpkin purée, cream, vanilla, cinnamon, ginger, cloves and salt. Mix with a spatula, or the mixer's paddle attachment on low speed, until well blended.

Take the crust out of the fridge and place on a baking tray. Spoon the filling into the crust. Bake in the oven for 15 minutes before reducing the temperature to 190°C and continuing to bake for 35–45 minutes or until a skewer inserted in the centre of the pie comes out clean. Remove from the oven and allow the pie to cool completely.

Combine all the cream cream ingredients in a bowl and whip to a smooth consistency. Slice the cooled pie, top with a big dollop of the cream cheese and cream cream and enjoy.

Chocolate Chip Cookie and Peanut Parfait Sandwiches

Ice cream sandwiches bring back so many memories for me. My dad's a big ice cream fan and more often than not during the summer school holidays this would be the go-to dessert. I've jazzed the original up a little with a parfait, which is easy to make and doesn't require a special ice-cream machine. The beauty of making your own is that you really can choose any flavour combination you like. I'm pretty standard and like the peanutty flavour with the gooey chocolate biscuit, but let your imagination run wild.

Preparation time: 6 hours (mostly setting time)

Cooking time: 10 minutes

Makes: 10

PEANUT PARFAIT

3 eggs

90g caster sugar

pinch of salt

pinch of nutmeg

pinch of cinnamon

120g peanuts

200ml cream

CHOCOLATE CHIP COOKIES

435g butter, softened

1¾ cups white sugar

2 eggs

2 teaspoons vanilla extract

2 cups plain flour

¾ cup cocoa

1 teaspoon baking powder

½ teaspoon salt

2 cups chocolate chips

Line a slice tin with plastic wrap, ensuring you have enough overhang to fold over the top of the tin.

Put the eggs, sugar, salt and spices in a glass or metallic bowl and place over a saucepan of simmering water. Whisk constantly until the mixture doubles in volume (about 3 minutes). Transfer the mixture to a cold bowl and place in the fridge to cool.

Whiz the nuts in a food processor until they resemble breadcrumbs. Whip the cream to soft peaks (don't overwhip it) and carefully fold in the nuts and the cooled egg mixture with a spatula. Pour the parfait mixture into the lined tin and cover with plastic wrap. Place in the freezer till set (5 hours or more).

For the cookies, cream the butter and sugar in a food processor till light and fluffy. Add the eggs and vanilla and process well. Add the flour, cocoa, baking powder and salt and blitz again till well blended. Finally, stir in the chocolate chips.

Remove the dough from the mixer and shape into balls about the size of golf balls. Place the dough balls in the fridge for 20 minutes.

Preheat the oven to 180°C. Line a couple of baking trays with baking paper.

Place the dough balls on the baking trays, allowing room for the biscuits to spread until doubled in size. Bake in the oven for 8–9 minutes. Remove from the oven and leave the cookies on the trays until cool. (The cookies will still be soft and fluffy but will harden slightly while cooling.)

To assemble, cut the parfait into squares roughly the size of the biscuits, removing each piece with a fish slice. Chuck a slice between two chocolate chip cookies and get stuck in.

Enjoying great food and good times with friends is priceless.

Custard Squares with Rhubarb

Man, oh man, custard squares make me weak at the knees and give me butterflies in my stomach. They remind me of summer trips to the dairy with my mates on our bikes. They would all go for ice cream but I'd always find it tough to go past the yellow squares of perfection. Rhubarb on the other hand has taken me a while to buy into but now I love the stuff. Give it to me in pies, on ice cream or just by itself with a little dollop of cream or yoghurt. I've combined the two here in a classic Kiwi custard square with a rhubarb icing that pairs perfectly with the vanilla. I'm yet to stop making them on the weekends — good luck to you!

Preparation time: 25 minutes

Cooking time: 25 minutes

Makes 10

CUSTARD SQUARES

300g frozen puff pastry sheets, thawed

2½ cups milk

100g butter

1⅓ cups cornflour

½ cup icing sugar

1 egg

1 teaspoon vanilla extract

RHUBARB ICING

50g caster sugar

¼ cup water

150g rhubarb, roughly chopped

1 cup icing sugar

Preheat the oven to 210°C. Line a square cake tin with baking paper, leaving enough hanging over the sides to help you lift out the squares.

Roll out 2 sheets of the pastry on baking paper to about 2–3mm thick. Cut the sheets roughly a quarter bigger than the tin you intend to use to assemble the custard squares. Prick the pastry all over with a skewer, then slide it, using the baking paper, on to baking trays. Pop in the oven for 10–12 minutes or until golden brown and cooked through. Remove from the oven and leave the pastry to cool on the trays while you make the custard.

Heat 2 cups of the milk with the butter in a medium-sized saucepan until the butter has melted. Mix the cornflour, icing sugar, egg and vanilla to a smooth paste with the remaining milk. Pour a small amount of the butter and milk mixture into the egg and sugar paste, stirring well. Then add this mixture back to the pan with the warm milk and butter. Cook the custard over a medium heat until it coats the back of a spoon, stirring constantly with a spatula. Leave the custard until cool.

Place 1 sheet of cooked pastry in the lined tin and fill with all of the cool custard. Place the other pastry sheet on top and press down lightly so the custard sticks to both sheets. Pop in the fridge until the icing is ready.

Place the caster sugar and water in a small saucepan over a low heat, and stir until the sugar has dissolved. Add the rhubarb to the pan and increase the heat to medium-high to bring to a boil. Once the mixture comes to a boil, reduce the heat to low and simmer for 10 minutes. Take the mixture off the heat and allow it to cool before stirring in the icing sugar. Spread the icing over the cooled custard square, then return the dish to the fridge for another 20 minutes till the icing has set. Lift the custard square out of the baking dish with the overhanging paper and cut into squares with a sharp knife.

Hot Cross Bun Panna Cotta with Rummy Raisins

Dad was the king of hot cross buns, and one of my favourite food memories is coming home after school in the months before Easter to freshly glazed buns, still sticky and hot, straight from the oven. This dessert is a nod to those memories, the scrummy sweet of a hot cross bun and the little bit of naughty from the rummy raisins, a match which really is heavenly.

Preparation time: 30 minutes plus setting time

Cooking time: 10 minutes

Feeds: 4

HOT CROSS BUN PANNA COTTA

2 cups cream

2 cups milk

6 tablespoons caster sugar

½ cup raisins

1 cinnamon stick

1 apple, finely diced

peel of ½ orange

1 slice peeled ginger

¼ teaspoon ground allspice

½ teaspoon vanilla extract

¼ teaspoon ground nutmeg

pinch of salt

3 teaspoons powdered gelatin

RUMMY RAISINS

½ cup raisins

¼ cup dark rum

100g butter

1 cup brown sugar

230ml cream

pinch of salt

Grease 4 ramekins with a neutral-flavoured oil.

Place the cream, milk, caster sugar, raisins, cinnamon stick, apple, orange peel and ginger in a saucepan over a medium heat until the sugar melts and the mixture begins to bubble round the sides of the pan. Remove immediately from the heat.

Place the allspice, vanilla, nutmeg, salt and gelatin in a large bowl and mix well. Stir in about 1 cup of the cream and fruit mixture and mix until well incorporated. Add the remaining cream mixture, stir well and leave to cool on the bench for 40 minutes.

Drain the cooled mixture through a sieve and into a jug, discarding the solids. Pour the panna cotta into the ramekins and place in the freezer for 1 hour. Stir the cold liquid, then place in the fridge for a further 4 hours or until set.

Soak the raisins in the rum for 10 minutes, then drain, reserving the rum. Melt the butter and sugar in a medium-sized saucepan over a medium heat, then add the raisins, cream and salt. Bring to the boil, then lower the heat and stir in the reserved rum. Allow to cool.

Trace round the outside of the set panna cotta with a small knife and turn out on to plates. Drizzle each pudding with a couple of spoonfuls of rummy raisin syrup and serve immediately.

Golden Syrup Dumplings

These sweet little angels are so tasty everyone will be reaching for them and dipping their fingers in the sauce afterwards. I like to serve them with plain yoghurt, pistachios and a little lemon zest, but let your imagination go crazy: ice cream, custard, milk, curd, fruit, chocolate – pretty much anything that goes with sugar can go with these guys.

Preparation time: 20 minutes

Cooking time: 25 minutes

Feeds: 6

3⅔ cups water

300g butter

1½ cups brown sugar

1⅔ cups golden syrup

1 cup milk

1½ cups self-raising flour

1 cup plain yoghurt to serve

zest of 1 lemon to serve

½ cup pistachios, crushed to serve

Pour the water into a large saucepan with half the butter, the sugar and ⅓ cup of the golden syrup. Bring to the boil over a medium-high heat. Once boiling, turn the heat down immediately so the mixture is just simmering.

Warm the milk in the microwave for 10 seconds.

Process the flour and the rest of the butter in a food processor until the mixture resembles breadcrumbs. Add 2 tablespoons of the golden syrup and the warmed milk and whiz until it comes together to form a dough.

Bring the syrup in the pan back to the boil and drop in spoonfuls of the dough. Turn the heat down to low and simmer for 10 minutes, turning the dumplings twice. You will probably need to cook the dumplings in batches, so scoop out the first lot and place in a baking dish with a little of the syrup. Cover with tin foil and keep warm while you cook the remaining dumplings.

Spoon a couple of dumplings into a bowl with a few spoonfuls of syrup. Drizzle over the yoghurt and top with lemon zest and pistachios.

Tequila Hardman Doughnuts

Tequila hardman shots have always intrigued me little, probably because of the thought that if you conquer them you're a hardman. This idea came during a mad rush in the *MasterChef* pantry when I saw a bottle of tequila out of the corner of my eye. It stuck with me a little and I thought that if I could incorporate tequila into a dish I'd get a few points for originality and bold flavours. And so this idea for dunking fluffy doughnuts into a curd that will punch you right in the kisser was born. Perfect for a night in, watching some sport or a good movie.

Preparation time: 25 minutes plus proving time

Cooking time: 10 minutes

Makes: 15–20

DOUGHNUTS

1½ teaspoons active dried yeast

¾ cup milk, warmed

1½ cups caster sugar

1 large egg, at room temperature

1 teaspoon vanilla extract

2 tablespoons water

2½ cups plain flour

½ teaspoon salt

4 tablespoons butter, melted

TEQUILA AND LIME CURD

1 cup sugar

5 tablespoons butter

⅔ cup lime juice

3–4 tablespoons tequila

zest of 2 limes

5 egg yolks

GLAZE

1½ cups icing sugar

3 tablespoons milk

2 teaspoons vanilla extract

1 litre canola oil for deep-frying

Place the yeast, warmed milk and 2 teaspoons of the caster sugar in a small bowl. Leave until foamy (about 5 minutes). Whisk the egg, vanilla and water in a separate bowl. Combine the flour, salt and remaining sugar in the bowl of a cake mixer fitted with the paddle attachment. Mixing on low speed, add the yeast mixture, egg mixture and melted butter and mix until just combined. Switch to a dough hook and knead on medium speed until the dough forms a ball and pulls away from the sides of the bowl (about 20 minutes). Place the dough in a large, greased bowl and cover with plastic wrap. Pop the dough in the fridge for at least a couple of hours or overnight if you can (the longer you leave it, the lighter the doughnuts).

For the curd, place the sugar and butter in a glass or metallic bowl over a saucepan of simmering water. Stir until the butter is melted. Remove from the heat and whisk in the lime juice, tequila and zest. Place the egg yolks in another bowl and whisk a little of the butter mixture into the yolks. Then whisk all the egg yolk mixture into the butter mixture (this stops the yolks from cooking – a process called tempering). Place the bowl back over the pan and heat, whisking constantly, for 10 minutes, or until the curd has thickened and coats the back of a spoon. Strain the curd through a sieve into a bowl and cover with plastic wrap, letting it sit directly on the surface of the curd. Pop the curd into the fridge to cool. It will thicken more as it cools.

For the glaze, sift the icing sugar into a medium-sized bowl. Slowly stir in the milk and vanilla until the mixture is smooth. If the glaze isn't smooth stir in an additional tablespoon of milk. Cover the glaze with plastic wrap and set it aside while you make the doughnut holes.

Scoop the dough into a piping bag with a large nozzle. (I sometimes improvise with a large zip-lock bag.)

Fill a heavy-based saucepan or deep-fryer with the canola oil and heat it to 170°C or just before smoking point. Line a baking tray with paper towels.

Recipe continued over page . . .

For each doughnut squeeze 2cm of dough out of the piping bag and carefully cut it off with wet scissors so it drops into the oil. Alternatively, using a couple of spoons, shape the dough into quenelles (an oval like a football) and gently drop into the oil.
Fry until golden brown (about 2 minutes), moving the doughnuts around as they cook. Transfer the cooked doughnuts to the paper towels to drain and cool briefly. Place a wire rack over some baking paper then, one by one, dip the doughnut holes into the glaze and transfer them to the rack to allow the excess glaze to drip off.

Dunk into the curd.

Raspberry and Pistachio Semifreddo

If you were to take this dessert to a dinner party everyone would think you were Nigella, but really you could have the cooking ability of Kermit the Frog. This semifreddo looks stunning, is big enough for a party but is as simple as a dessert comes — trust me, I can do it!

Preparation time: 30 minutes

Freezing time: about 8 hours

Feeds: 4

½ cup pistachios

2 cups fresh or frozen raspberries

¾ cup caster sugar

3 egg yolks

1½ cups cream

½ teaspoon vanilla extract

fresh mint leaves to serve

Line a loaf tin with plastic wrap, ensuring you have enough overhang to fold over the top of the tin.

Pulse the pistachios in a food processor to rough chunks.

Place the raspberries and ¼ cup of the caster sugar in a food processor and blend to a purée. Strain through a sieve into a bowl.

Place the egg yolks and remaining sugar in a glass or metallic bowl over a saucepan of simmering water. Whisk until tripled in volume and pale in colour (about 3 minutes). Sit the bowl in another bowl of iced water and continue to whisk until the mixture is cool (about another 3 minutes).

Beat the cream and vanilla until soft peaks form. Whisk a third of the cream mixture into the egg mixture until smooth, then fold in the remaining cream mixture.

Stir half the semifreddo into the raspberry purée and pour it into the loaf tin. Stir the pistachios through the other half of the mixture and gently pour on top of the raspberry cream. Fold the plastic wrap over the top of the tin and place in the freezer until frozen (at least 8 hours).

Unwrap the semifreddo and turn out on to a serving platter. Remove the plastic wrap and cut into slices for people to dig in. Garnish with fresh mint leaves.

the basics

Tim's Mayo

Preparation time: 5 minutes

Makes: approximately 1½ cups

1 egg

juice of 1 small lemon

1 teaspoon Dijon mustard

salt and pepper

¾ cup grapeseed oil

This is a super-simple, quick mayonnaise recipe that can be used as the base for so many other sauces. It's combined with a few different bits and pieces in this cookbook but don't let that limit you. Go crazy and have fun. If you want a flavoured mayo, add herbs, spices, vinegars or even purées at the end, but avoid flavoured or infused oils as this makes the mayo taste a little rank. I use grapeseed oil because it is unflavoured and high in unsaturated fats (the good type). Another option is canola oil for the same reasons. Also, the amount of oil stated is just a guideline for the thickness I like. If you would like a runnier mayo, use less oil, and for a thicker mayo, use more — it's that simple.

Combine the egg, lemon juice, Dijon mustard and a little salt and pepper in a large bowl.

The oil has to be slowly poured in while the mayonnaise is being constantly mixed. An easy way to do this is with a stick blender. Slowly drizzle the oil into the mixture with the blender on full speed. Stop drizzling in the oil when the mayonnaise reaches your desired consistency.

The old-fashioned way takes a little longer and uses a little more elbow grease but is far more enjoyable. Place the bowl on a folded tea towel (this will stop the bowl sliding) and drizzle in the oil while you whisk. You may need to stop at times to make sure the oil isn't collecting in a big pool. Keep whisking in the oil until the mayo is at the desired consistency.

Season to taste with salt and pepper. Pour into a jar and store in the fridge for a couple of weeks.

Pizza
Dough

Preparation time: 30 minutes

Cooking time: 8–10 minutes

Makes: 4 medium-sized bases

1½ teaspoons active dried yeast

½ tablespoon caster sugar

320ml warm water

2⅔ cups high-grade flour

⅔ cup semolina flour

½ tablespoon salt

This dough is the stuff of legends. I always wanted to be able to make the thin, crispy bases that you get at restaurants with wood-fired pizza ovens — then I learnt the trick was a good, stretchy dough. Roll these guys out as thin as you can to make sure they go crispy, as they will puff up a little. To make the base super fine you could just use semolina flour, but I like this combination the best. If you don't have semolina flour on hand just use high-grade.

Mix the yeast and sugar into the warm water and leave for 5 minutes until foamy. Tip the flours on to a clean bench and add the salt. Make a well in the flour and pour the yeast mixture into the well. Starting from the inside use a fork to slowly draw in the flour, mixing until the dough begins to come together. Now ditch the fork and with your hands begin to shape the dough into a ball. Knead the dough for 5 minutes or until soft and springy. Dust the dough in a little flour, cover in plastic wrap and let it rest for 20 minutes at room temperature.

Divide the dough into 4 equal portions and roll out on a clean bench to the desired thickness and width. Move the bases to a baking tray and top with toppings.

Preheat the oven to 190°C and cook until the bases are crispy underneath (the cooking time depends on thickness of the base but should be 7–10 minutes).

Silky Smooth Pasta

Preparation time: 40 minutes

Feeds: 4 people

250g 00 flour

2 eggs

1 egg yolk (reserve the white in case you need it)

pinch of salt

Making your own pasta is one of the most rewarding jobs you'll ever do in a kitchen. It takes a little effort but the results are worth it, ten-fold. Using an extra egg yolk makes the pasta that much richer in flavour and also gives it a really nice colour. Do keep the remaining egg white — because eggs differ so much in size you may need a small amount to help to bring the dough together. Keep in mind that you may not need it; while the dough may initially feel dry and hard, with a good amount of working it will come out silky smooth and stretchy.

Sift the flour into a large bowl and add the remaining ingredients. Stir in circles with your hands, gradually combining the egg and flour to form a dough. Turn the dough out on to a dry bench and knead until the dough starts to come together. In terms of kneading technique, just try to find your own. Squash it into the table, roll it, squash and stretch again seems to be mine, but it really only takes a bit of elbow grease and force. You'll know when you've done enough kneading when the dough is silky smooth all over and has a little bit of stretch in it. Cover the dough in plastic wrap and place in the fridge for at least 30 minutes.

Now it's time to roll the dough out; a pasta machine makes this a lot easier but it can be done with a rolling pin if the dough is broken down into many smaller pieces. Take a look at your recipe to see what shape and how thick the pasta needs to be before you start the rolling process.

Remove the dough from the fridge and turn it out on to a well-floured bench. Knead for a few minutes until you feel the stretch come back into the dough. Cut the dough into 3 pieces and cover 2 with the plastic wrap.

Shape the dough into a flat pancake and pass it through the machine on its highest setting. Dust the dough with flour, fold it in half and pass it through the machine again. I repeat this process maybe 5–6 times as this helps to get the pasta super smooth; you will notice the difference in texture each time you do it.

Now begin to roll the pasta down through the settings, getting the dough thinner and thinner each time. If the dough sticks to the machine at all, dust it with a little flour, fold it in half and repeat the same setting. Take the pasta down to the required thickness and cut to shape.

Dust the pasta with a little 00 flour to stop it sticking together before working the other 2 pieces of dough.

Slider Buns

This recipe is for patient people. Rush the proving period and the buns will be dense, but let them rest and they will be the lightest buns you've ever had. Feel free to add seeds to the top of the buns. I'm a big fan of sesame but experiment away.

Preparation time: 4 hours 20 minutes

Cooking time: 10 minutes

Makes: 8 buns

1 cup warm water

3 tablespoons warm milk

2 teaspoons active dried yeast

2½ tablespoons sugar

3 cups high-grade flour

⅓ cup plain flour

1½ teaspoons salt

35g unsalted butter, softened

2 large eggs

sesame seeds or poppy seeds to sprinkle (optional)

Combine the warm water, warm milk, yeast and sugar in a small bowl. Leave for 5 minutes until the mixture becomes foamy.

Place the flours, salt and butter in the bowl of an electric mixer. Using the paddle attachment, mix on medium speed until the butter is the size of crumbs.

Stir in the yeast mixture and 1 beaten egg. Mix on medium-low speed until a dough forms (8–10 minutes). The dough is meant to be sticky and wet and hold together well. Don't be tempted to add more flour.

Shape the dough into a ball and place in a bowl covered with a clean, damp tea towel. Let the dough rise in a warm place until doubled in size. This can take anywhere from 1–3 hours, depending on the temperature.

Line a tray with baking paper. Using a well-floured knife, divide the dough into 8 equal portions. Shape the dough into balls on a well-floured bench. First, very gently flatten each piece like a pancake. Pull up each side, pinching the dough together in the centre until it's shaped like a ball. Flip the ball over, pinched side down, and place on an unfloured part of the bench (it's easier to roll this way). Using your palm, gently roll into a smooth ball. Transfer to the baking tray, leaving enough room for each dough ball to expand by half. Cover loosely with plastic wrap and let the buns rise in a warm place for another hour, or until puffy and slightly risen.

If you want hotdog-shaped rolls flatten each piece like a pancake again. Fold the circle in half, then in half in the same direction again. Tuck the ends under the roll and place on a baking tray, leaving enough room for each dough roll to expand by half. Cover loosely with plastic wrap and leave to rise in a warm place for another hour, or until puffy and slightly risen.

Preheat the oven to 200°C. Place an oven tray in the bottom of the oven with a shallow layer of water in it. The steam this produces will keep the buns moist while they cook.

To make the egg wash, beat the remaining egg with a splash of water. When the buns have finished rising, gently brush each one with egg wash. If you're going to add seeds, now would be the time.

Bake the buns for 10–15 minutes or until golden brown. Transfer to a wire rack to cool completely.

Guasacaca

Preparation time: 10 minutes

Makes: 2 cups

2 ripe avocados, roughly chopped

1 small brown onion, roughly chopped

1 small green capsicum, roughly chopped

1 medium jalapeño, deseeded and roughly chopped (optional)

2 medium cloves garlic, roughly chopped

½ cup roughly chopped fresh coriander leaves

¼ cup roughly chopped fresh flat-leaf parsley leaves

¼ cup white vinegar

juice of 1 lime

⅓ cup olive oil

salt and freshly ground black pepper

Guasacaca is the Venezuelan version of guacamole. It has a bit of punch from the chilli and, because it's an purée, it has a little more of a sauce texture. Perfect on tacos, barbecued beef or chicken, or any spicy stew like the chilli con carne on page 48.

Place all the ingredients except the olive oil in a food processor. Pulse until well minced.

With the motor running, drizzle in the olive oil and process until the sauce is completely smooth.

Season with salt and pepper. Transfer to a bowl and serve immediately.

Flat Breads or Naan

Preparation time: 15 minutes

Cooking time: 2–3 minutes each side

Makes: 6 breads

400g yoghurt

400g plain flour, plus more for dusting

1 heaped teaspoon baking powder

pinch of salt

I learnt this flat bread recipe from a couple of people in the *MasterChef* house. At the time I was pretty hungry so I managed to steal some of the dough and wrapped up some pancetta and mozzarella and then dry-fried it. It was one of the best things I tasted in the house. A wee toasted wrap made out of this dough could be filled with anything, so fill your boots: some minced garlic, finely chopped coriander or parsley and a small knob of butter makes a pretty good naan. Or plain flat breads go brilliantly with the curry recipes on pages 62 and 92.

Combine all the ingredients in a big bowl or in the bowl of an electric mixer. Mix with the dough hook on medium speed until a dough forms. Alternatively, combine all the ingredients in a large bowl and, using a wooden spoon, mix until it forms an even dough with no lumps.

Tip the dough on to a floured bench and knead for 1–2 minutes. Split the dough in half, return 1 piece to the bowl and cover with plastic wrap or a plate. Roll the other half out until approximately 5mm thick, or to your desired thickness – remember it will rise slightly. Repeat with the remaining dough.

If you're making flat bread for a curry recipe then separate the dough into 6 equal pieces and roll them out thinly, storing them on a plate with baking paper between each one.

Cook in a dry frying pan on a medium heat until lightly browned on one side (about 2 minutes), then flip and cook until crispy. Once crispy on the second side, set aside on a serving plate, place in a warm oven and repeat with the rest of the dough circles.

Carolina Rub Mix

Preparation time: 5 minutes

Makes: about ½ cup

2 tablespoons smoked paprika

1 tablespoon black pepper

1 tablespoon salt

1 tablespoon cayenne pepper

1 tablespoon chilli powder

1 tablespoon ground coriander

1 tablespoon brown sugar

This rub has a beautiful kick and smokiness. It's perfect on just about any protein but on pork, chicken and fish it is crazy good.

Mix all the ingredients together and store in an airtight container until ready to use.

Pie Crust

This is a truly classic American pie crust. This guy can be used with any sweet pie filling and can be blind-baked before using if that's what is required.

Preparation time: 1 hour
20 minutes

Makes: 1 x 23cm pie crust

2½ cups high-grade flour

1 teaspoon salt

1 tablespoon caster sugar

230g ice-cold butter

6–8 tablespoons ice-cold water

Place 1½ cups of the flour with the salt and sugar in a food processor. Pulse 2–3 times until combined. Cut the butter into even-sized cubes, scatter them over the flour and process until a dough or paste begins to form (about 30 seconds). Scrape the sides of the bowl down so the dough is all on the base, then add the remaining flour. Pulse 4–5 times until the dough is an even texture and looks broken up and a little crumbly.

Transfer the mixture to a medium-sized bowl and sprinkle over 6 tablespoons of the ice-cold water. Using a spatula, press the dough into itself. The crumbs should begin to come together. If you pinch some of the dough and it holds together, it's ready. If the dough falls apart, add 1 more tablespoon of water and continue to press until the dough comes together. Repeat with another tablespoon of water if required.

Tip the dough out on to a clean bench. Work the dough just enough to form a ball, but do not overwork otherwise the dough might be a little dense. Flatten into a thick pancake and wrap in plastic wrap. Pop in the fridge for at least 1 hour or even a few days. Remove the dough from the fridge and roll it to your desired thickness and size.

Barbecue Sauce

Preparation time: 5 minutes

Cooking time: 20 minutes

Makes: 1½ cups

olive oil for cooking

1 small red onion, finely chopped

3 cloves garlic, finely chopped

2 teaspoons smoked paprika

1 teaspoon ground fennel

3 teaspoons red wine vinegar

2 tablespoons maple syrup (honey or brown sugar would be fine here too)

6 tablespoons tomato ketchup

3 tablespoons water

juice of ½ lemon

salt and pepper

Everyone loves a good barbecue sauce and this one is up there. I don't like the intense sweetness of the storebought sauces so being able to control that myself is really nice. Smash this guy on any kind of sandwich, anything with chicken or bacon, or try it with my ribs recipe on page 16. It keeps for a few weeks in the fridge so store it for later and you'll find yourself making trips to the fridge just to dip your finger in.

Heat a splash of olive oil in a large saucepan over a medium-high heat. Add the onion and garlic and cook until softened (about 8 minutes).

Stir in the paprika and ground fennel and cook for 5 minutes until dry and fragrant, then add the vinegar and maple syrup. Mix well and cook for 2 minutes.

Finally add the ketchup, water and lemon juice, then turn the heat down to low and leave the sauce to reduce for 10 minutes so it becomes nice and sticky. Season with salt and pepper. Pour the sauce into a bowl, cover and pop in the fridge. This should keep for a couple of weeks.

Tartare
Sauce

This sauce is one of those things that gets better with age. If you're able to make it a few hours beforehand the flavour is good; if you leave it for a few days, the flavour is exceptional. For the salt-baked snapper (see page 122) I like to make quite a chunky tartare sauce, but if that's not your style then just cut everything up more finely.

Preparation time: 5 minutes

Makes: 1½ cups

3 tablespoons capers, drained and chopped

3 tablespoons chopped gherkins

1 small shallot, finely chopped

3 tablespoons chopped fresh flat-leaf parsley

juice of 1 lemon

¾ cup Tim's mayo (see page 150)

salt and freshly ground black pepper

Combine the capers, gherkins, shallot, parsley and lemon juice. Stir in the mayo and season with salt and pepper. Pour the sauce into a bowl and set aside until it's time to serve.

Tortillas or Soft Tacos

Preparation time: 25 minutes

Cooking time: 2 minutes
each side

Makes: 14–20

3 cups plain flour

1 teaspoon salt

1 teaspoon baking powder

⅓ cup vegetable oil

1 cup warm water

This little guy differs from the flat bread in that it doesn't rise at all so is perfect for wraps, tacos and tortillas. Just roll these out to your desired size and number and dry-fry. This mixture does make a lot of dough but reducing the volume of ingredients gets a bit tricky – trust me, I've tried – but you can store the cooked breads in a zip-lock bag or freeze them to be dragged out at another time.

Place the flour, salt and baking powder in the bowl of an electric mixer. Mix with the dough hook on a low speed until combined. Add the oil and water with the mixer running on medium speed. Mix for 30-second intervals, 3–4 times, stopping to scrape down the sides of the bowl, until the the mixture comes together and forms a ball. Turn the speed back down to low and continue to mix for 1 minute or until the dough is smooth. This dough can also be mixed by hand – follow the same instructions and ensure the dough is of an even consistency before adding oil and water.

Tip the dough out on to a well-floured bench. Divide the dough into 14–16 equal-sized portions (around 20 for tacos). Roll each portion into a ball, then flatten with the palm of your hand, using more flour if the dough gets a little sticky. Allow the flattened dough balls to rest under a tea towel for about 15 minutes.

Heat a large frying pan over a medium-high heat. Lightly flour the bench and a rolling pin and roll each dough piece into a rough circle. Don't stack the rolled out breads or they'll stick together. When the pan is hot, place in a tortilla and cook for about 2 minutes or until the underside has a few pale brown spots. Flip and cook for another 2 minutes. Repeat for all the other portions. Keep warm, then serve immediately.

Basil Pesto

Preparation time: 10 minutes

Makes: 1½ cups

1 small clove garlic, roughly chopped

1 teaspoon sea salt

1 teaspoon black pepper

3 good handfuls of fresh basil leaves, roughly chopped

1 cup pine nuts

½ cup grated Parmesan

¼ cup olive oil

juice of ½ lemon

This is a straightforward basil pesto for the stuffed chicken breast recipe on page 64. However, you can be as crazy as you like with the ingredients and just use the recipe for reference. If you want watercress or parsley in there, chuck in the same quantity as the basil! If you want to use walnuts, use them! Just be aware of how oily each type of nut is, as you may need to add a little more olive oil to get the same consistency. I've made this mixture in a mortar and pestle as I find you get better results with bashing the basil than blending. However, it can be done in a food processor; just follow the same steps and follow your nose.

Pound the garlic with the salt, pepper and basil leaves in a mortar and pestle. Toss in the pine nuts and pound again. Mix through half of the Parmesan and, while stirring, drizzle in half of the olive oil. Then add the remaining cheese and the oil. Add the lemon juice and season to taste. Refrigerate until required. The pesto will keep for up to a week in the fridge.

Ranch Dressing

Preparation time: 10 minutes

Makes: 1 cup

1 clove garlic, minced

½ cup buttermilk

2 tablespoons sour cream

2 tablespoons mayo

½ teaspoon white wine vinegar

small bunch of chives, finely sliced

salt and pepper

This is the dipping sauce for the buffalo wings on page 66 but the dressing could easily go on a potato or pasta salad or with hot chips and roasties. Its freshness cuts through either really spicy or starchy ingredients. It'll keep well in the fridge too; just cover it tightly with plastic wrap and it will keep for a couple of weeks.

Place the garlic, buttermilk, sour cream, mayo and white wine vinegar in a food processor and mix on high speed for a couple of minutes. Stir through the chives and season with salt and pepper.

Mint Sauce

Preparation time: 2 hours (infusing time)

Cooking time: 7 minutes

Makes: 2–3 roasts' worth

6 tablespoons water

4 tablespoons caster sugar

4 tablespoons malt vinegar

handful of mint leaves, finely chopped

A real Kiwi classic, this one. The taste of artificial mint used to make me feel ill, to the point where I used neutral-flavoured toothpaste. This was all prior to me properly discovering fresh mint though, and the difference between fresh mint and artificial is immense. I prefer to make my own mint sauce because of this, and creating a refreshing sauce for some hearty lamb is what makes a roast for me. This guy can last in the fridge for 3–4 weeks but straight after the 2-hour resting time is when it's at its best.

Combine the water and sugar in a small saucepan over a medium-high heat. Bring to a simmer and continue to simmer until syrupy (3–5 minutes). Remove from the heat, add the malt vinegar and pour into a small bowl. Allow to cool a little, then stir through the mint. Cover and place in the fridge for at least 2 hours before using – this allows the mint oils to infuse the sauce.

acknowledgements

This book is the result of the collective effort of so many talented and supportive people. I must acknowledge Jenny Hellen and the team at Allen & Unwin — it's my first time taking on such an adventure, and it has been amazing to complete it with such a proficient team. To the others involved, Kimberley Davis, Tam West and Vic Bell, your professionalism and skill has made this book what it is, and I am so thankful for your hard work and generosity of knowledge and expertise.

A massive thank you to Sally and Harmony meats for supplying the proteins for this book, and also to Aaron Styles and Just Another Fisherman not only for the gear but also for the support. I want to recognise the work of my agent, Belinda Foster: she has brilliantly captured who I am as a person and has helped me to communicate that in this book.

Throughout this book I've mentioned a few people who are special to me, all of whom have supported my journey in one way or another. I would also like to mention Johnny and Bex for their support, wisdom and encouragement through a such a life-changing season.

Lastly I would like to thank the Creator because without Him, none of this would be possible.

index

A

artichokes
  Pancetta, Mushroom, Artichoke
    Heart and Olive Pizza 32
Aunty Anna's Banana Cake 126
avocado
  Chilli Con Carne with Guasacaca
    and Corn Muffins 48
  Guasacaca 180

B

bacon
  Bacon Hock, Cress and Pine Nut
    Ravioli 30
  Seafood Spaghetti with Bacon, Leek
    and Caramelised Fennel 112
baking
  Aunty Anna's Banana Cake 126
  Chocolate Chip Cookie and Peanut
    Parfait Sandwiches 132
  Corn Muffins 48
  Custard Squares with Rhubarb 136
  Flat Breads or Naan 162
  Never-fail Chocolate Cake with
    Chocolate Praline Ganache 128
  Pie Crust 166
  Pizza Dough 152
  Pumpkin Pie with Cream Cheese
    and Cream Cream 130
  Slider Buns 156
  Soft Tacos 174
  Tortillas 174
balsamic
  Garlic Butter Chicken Salad with
    Cranberry Balsamic Sauce 54
  Pesto-stuffed Chicken Breast with
    Balsamic Pasta Salad 64
banana cake, Aunty Anna's 126
Barbecue Sauce 168
basil
  Basil Pesto 176

  Pesto-stuffed Chicken Breast with
    Balsamic Pasta Salad 64
  Schnitzel Dogs with Tomato,
    Mozzarella and Basil 46
beans
  Chicken Tacos with Refried Beans
    and Corn Salsa 70
  Jerk Chicken with Jamaican Rice
    and Peas 72
Beef Shin Cobbler 50
Beet and Pecan Salad (with venison
  steaks) 84
Bone Marrow with Salsa Verde and
  Crusty Bread 36
bread
  Bone Marrow with Salsa Verde and
    Crusty Bread 36
  Flat Breads or Naan 162
  Slider Buns 156
  Tortillas or Soft Tacos 174
Brussels sprouts
  Dry Red Duck Curry 78
Buffalo Wings with Ranch Dressing
  66
burgers and buns see also
  sandwiches
  Ginger Beer Tempura Oyster Sliders
    with Japanese Slaw 118
  Pulled Pork Sliders 24
  Schnitzel Dogs with Tomato,
    Mozzarella and Basil 46
  Slider Buns 156

C

cakes
  Aunty Anna's Banana Cake 126
  Never-fail Chocolate Cake with
    Chocolate Praline Ganache 128
Carolina Rub Mix 164
Cauliflower and Horseradish Mash
  (with roast beef) 44

Celeriac Remoulade (with roast lamb)
  100
Chicken Meatballs with Chinese
  Noodle Soup 74
Chicken Tacos with Refried Beans
  and Corn Salsa 70
Chicken Tikka 58
Chicken Tikka Masala 62
Chilli Con Carne with Guasacaca and
  Corn Muffins 48
Chilli Corn (with pork enchiladas) 28
Chinese Noodle Soup (with chicken
  meatballs) 74
chips, parsnip (with crispy salmon)
  106
chocolate
  Chocolate Chip Cookie and Peanut
    Parfait Sandwiches 132
  Never-fail Chocolate Cake with
    Chocolate Praline Ganache 128
cobbler, beef shin 50
Confit Pork Belly with Spicy Fig Sauce
  18
cookies
  Chocolate Chip Cookie and Peanut
    Parfait Sandwiches 132
corn
  Chilli Corn (with pork enchiladas)
    28
  Corn Muffins (with chilli con carne)
    48
  Corn Salsa (with chicken tacos) 70
couscous, pineapple sage (with roast
  chicken) 56
cranberries
  Garlic Butter Chicken Salad with
    Cranberry Balsamic Sauce 54
crayfish sandwich (with malt mayo
  slaw) 104
cream
  Pumpkin Pie with Cream Cheese
    and Cream Cream 130

cream cheese
    Pumpkin Pie with Cream Cheese
        and Cream Cream 130
Creamy Paua on Toast 110
cress
    Bacon Hock, Cress and Pine Nut
        Ravioli 30
Crispy Salmon with Middle Eastern
    Parsnip Chips and Mint Pistachio
    Pesto 106
curd, tequila and lime 142
curries
    Chicken Tikka Masala 62
    Dry Red Duck Curry 78
    Lamb Andhra Curry 92
Custard Squares with Rhubarb 136

D

Dijon mustard
    Lamb Rack with Baby Potatoes and
        Dijonnaise 94
doughnuts, tequila hardman 142
dressings see also sauces
    Korean Chilli Dressing 38
    Ranch Dressing 178
    Tim's Mayo 150
    Wasabi Mayo 118
Dry Red Duck Curry 78
duck
    Dry Red Duck Curry 78
    Duck, Fig and Hoisin Pizza 80
dumplings (golden syrup) 140

E

enchiladas, pork (with chilli corn) 28

F

fennel
    Prawn, Fennel, Onion and Lemon
        Pizza 114
    Seafood Spaghetti with Bacon, Leek
        and Caramelised Fennel 112
figs
    Confit Pork Belly with Spicy Fig
        Sauce 18
    Duck, Fig and Hoisin Pizza 80
fish, salt-baked (with green beans)
    122
Flat Breads or Naan 162

G

Garlic Butter Chicken Salad with
    Cranberry Balsamic Sauce 54
Ginger Beer Tempura Oyster Sliders
    with Japanese Slaw 118
gravy (for roast beef) 44
green beans (with salt-baked fish) 122
Golden Syrup Dumplings 140
Guasacaca 160

H

hoisin
    Duck, Fig and Hoisin Pizza 80
horseradish and cauliflower mash
    (with roast beef) 44
Hot Cross Bun Panna Cotta with
    Rummy Raisins 138

I

Indian
    Chicken Tikka 58
    Chicken Tikka Masala 62
    Lamb Andhra Curry 92
Italian
    Bacon Hock, Cress and Pine Nut
        Ravioli 30
    Duck, Fig and Hoisin Pizza 80
    Lamb Neck Pappardelle 90
    Pancetta, Mushroom, Artichoke
        Heart and Olive Pizza 32
    Pesto-stuffed Chicken Breast with
        Balsamic Pasta Salad 64
    Prawn, Fennel, Onion and Lemon
        Pizza 114
    Seafood Spaghetti with Bacon, Leek
        and Caramelised Fennel 112

J

Jamaican
    Jerk Chicken with Jamaican Rice
        and Peas 72
Jerk Chicken with Jamaican Rice and
    Peas 72

K

kale
    Pork, Plum and Kale Salad 22
Korean Chilli Dressing 38

L

labneh, spiced (with lamb loin and
    roast pumpkin) 98
Lamb Andhra Curry 92
Lamb Loin with Roast Pumpkin and
    Spiced Labneh 98
Lamb Neck Pappardelle 90
Lamb Rack with Baby Potatoes and
    Dijonnaise 94
leeks
    Seafood Spaghetti with Bacon, Leek
        and Caramelised Fennel 112
lemons
    Prawn, Fennel, Onion and Lemon
        Pizza 114
lychees
    Dry Red Duck Curry 78

M

macadamias
    Never-fail Chocolate Cake with
        Chocolate Praline Ganache 128
Malt Mayo Slaw 104
mayo, Tim's 150
meatballs, chicken (with Chinese
    Noodle Soup) 74
Mexican
    Chicken Tacos with Refried Beans
        and Corn Salsa 70
    Chilli Con Carne with Guasacaca
        and Corn Muffins 48
    Pork Enchiladas with Chilli Corn 28
Middle Eastern Parsnip Chips 106
mint
    Mint Pistachio Pesto (with crispy
        salmon) 106
    Mint Sauce 180
mozzarella
    Duck, Fig and Hoisin Pizza 80
    Prawn, Fennel, Onion and Lemon
        Pizza 114
    Schnitzel Dogs with Tomato,
        Mozzarella and Basil 46
muffins, corn (with chilli con carne)
    48
mushrooms
    Pancetta, Mushroom, Artichoke
        Heart and Olive Pizza 32
    Roast Venison Loin with Polenta
        and Mushrooms 86

N

Naan 162
Never-fail Chocolate Cake with
   Chocolate Praline Ganache 128
noodle soup, chinese (with chicken
   meatballs) 74
nuts *see individual nuts*

O

olives
   Pancetta, Mushroom, Artichoke
      Heart and Olive Pizza 32
onions
   Prawn, Fennel, Onion and Lemon
      Pizza 114
   Onion Rings 58
oysters
   Ginger Beer Tempura Oyster Sliders
      with Japanese Slaw 118

P

Pancetta, Mushroom, Artichoke Heart
   and Olive Pizza 32
panna cotta, hot cross bun (with
   Rummy Raisins) 138
pappardelle, lamb neck 90
parfait
   Chocolate Chip Cookie and Peanut
      Parfait Sandwiches 132
parsnip chips (with crispy salmon) 106
pasta
   Bacon Hock, Cress and Pine Nut
      Ravioli 30
   Lamb Neck Pappardelle 90
   Pesto-stuffed Chicken Breast with
      Balsamic Pasta Salad 64
   Seafood Spaghetti with Bacon, Leek
      and Caramelised Fennel 112
   Silky Smooth Pasta 154
pastry
   Pie Crust 166
paua, creamy (on toast) 110
peanuts
   Chocolate Chip Cookie and Peanut
      Parfait Sandwiches 132
pecan and beet salad (with venison
   steaks) 84
pesto
   Basil Pesto 176
   Mint Pistachio Pesto (with crispy

salmon) 106
Pesto-stuffed Chicken Breast with
   Balsamic Pasta Salad 64
pies
   Pie Crust 166
   Pumpkin Pie with Cream Cheese
      and Cream Cream 130
pineapple
   Dry Red Duck Curry 78
   Roast Chicken with Pineapple Sage
      Couscous 56
pine nuts
   Bacon Hock, Cress and Pine Nut
      Ravioli 30
pistachios
   Crispy Salmon with Middle Eastern
      Parsnip Chips and Mint Pistachio
      Pesto 106
   Raspberry and Pistachio Semifreddo
      146
pizza
   Duck, Fig and Hoisin Pizza 80
   Pancetta, Mushroom, Artichoke
      Heart and Olive Pizza 32
   Pizza Dough 152
   Prawn, Fennel, Onion and Lemon
      Pizza 114
plums
   Pork, Plum and Kale Salad 22
Poached Crayfish Sandwich with Malt
   Mayo Slaw 104
polenta
   Roast Venison Loin with Polenta
      and Mushrooms 86
pork belly, confit (with spicy fig
   sauce) 18
Pork Enchiladas with Chilli Corn 28
Pork, Plum and Kale Salad 22
port
   Venison Steaks with Beet and Pecan
      Salad and Port Sauce 84
potatoes
   Crispy Potatoes 16
   Lamb Rack with Baby Potatoes and
      Dijonnaise 94
   Texan Salad (with spiced brisket) 40
Prawn, Fennel, Onion and Lemon
   Pizza 114
Pulled Pork Sliders 24
pumpkin
   Lamb Loin with Roast Pumpkin and
      Spiced Labneh 98

Pumpkin Pie with Cream Cheese
   and Cream Cream 130

R

raisins
   Hot Cross Bun Panna Cotta with
      Rummy Raisins 138
Ranch Dressing 178
Raspberry and Pistachio Semifreddo
   146
ravioli, bacon hock, cress and pine
   nut 30
Refried Beans (with chicken tacos)
   70
rhubarb
   Custard Squares with Rhubarb 136
ribs, smoky barbecue ribs (with crispy
   potatoes and slaw) 16
Rice and Peas, Jamaican (with jerk
   chicken) 72
Roast Beef with Cauliflower and
   Horseradish Mash and Gravy 44
Roast Chicken with Pineapple Sage
   Couscous 56
Roast Lamb with Celeriac Remoulade
   and Mint Sauce 100
Roast Venison Loin with Polenta and
   Mushrooms 86
rub mixes
   Carolina Rub Mix 164
   Jerk Rub 72
rum
   Hot Cross Bun Panna Cotta with
      Rummy Raisins 138

S

sage
   Roast Chicken with Pineapple Sage
      Couscous 56
salads and slaws
   Balsamic Pasta Salad 64
   Beet and Pecan Salad 84
   Garlic Butter Chicken Salad with
      Cranberry Balsamic Sauce 54
   Japanese Slaw 118
   Pork, Plum and Kale Salad 22
   Malt Mayo Slaw 104
   Skirt Steak Salad Wraps with Korean
      Chilli Dressing 38
   Slaw 16

Texan Salad 40
Thai Whitebait Salad 120
salmon, crispy (with parsnip chips
    and mint pistachio pesto) 106
salsas
    Corn salsa (with chicken tacos) 70
    Salsa Verde (with bone marrow) 36
Salt-baked Fish with Green Beans and
    Tartare Sauce 122
sandwiches *see also* burgers and
    buns
    Chocolate Chip Cookie and Peanut
        Parfait Sandwiches 132
    Creamy Paua on Toast 110
    Poached Crayfish Sandwich with
        Malt Mayo Slaw 104
sauces *see also* dressings
    Barbecue Sauce 168
    Buffalo Sauce 66
    Cranberry Balsamic Sauce 54
    Mint Sauce 180
    Port Sauce 84
    Salsa Verde 36
    Spicy Fig Sauce 18
    Tartare Sauce 170
    Yoghurt Dipping Sauce 58
Schnitzel Dogs with Tomato,
    Mozzarella and Basil 46
Seafood Spaghetti with Bacon, Leek
    and Caramelised Fennel 112
semifreddo, raspberry and pistachio
    146
Silky Smooth Pasta 154
Skirt Steak Salad Wraps with Korean
    Chilli Dressing 38
slaw
    Ginger Beer Tempura Oyster Sliders
        with Japanese Slaw 118
    Poached Crayfish Sandwich with
        Malt Mayo Slaw 104
    Smoky Barbecue Ribs with Crispy
        Potatoes and Slaw 16
Slider Buns 156
sliders *see* burgers and buns
Smoky Barbecue Ribs with Crispy
    Potatoes and Slaw 16
Soft Tacos 174
soup, Chinese noodle (with chicken
    meatballs) 74
spaghetti, seafood (with bacon, leek
    and caramelised fennel) 112
Spiced Brisket with Texan Salad 40

tacos
    Chicken Tacos with Refried Beans
        and Corn Salsa 70
    Tortillas or Soft Tacos 174
Tartare Sauce 170
tempura
    Ginger Beer Tempura Oyster Sliders
        with Japanese Slaw 118
Tequila and Lime Curd 142
Tequila Hardman Doughnuts 142
Thai
    Dry Red Duck Curry 78
    Thai Whitebait Salad 120
tikka, chicken 58
tikka masala, chicken 62
Tim's Mayo 150
tomatoes
    Schnitzel Dogs with Tomato,
        Mozzarella and Basil 46
Tortillas or Soft Tacos 174

venison
    Roast Venison Loin with Polenta
        and Mushrooms 86
    Venison Steaks with Beet and Pecan
        Salad and Port Sauce 84

W
Wasabi Mayo 118
whitebait salad, Thai 120
wings, buffalo (with ranch dressing)
    66
wraps
    Skirt Steak Salad Wraps with Korean
        Chilli Dressing 38

yoghurt
    Lamb Loin with Roast Pumpkin and
        Spiced Labneh 98
    Yoghurt Dipping Sauce 58

Allen & Unwin
Level 3, 228 Queen Street
Auckland 1010, New Zealand
Phone: (64 9) 377 3800
Email: info@allenandunwin.co.nz
Web: www.allenandunwin.com
83 Alexander Street
Crows Nest NSW 2065, Australia
Phone: (61 2) 8425 0100

A catalogue record for this book is available
from the National Library of New Zealand

ISBN 978 1 877505 68 3
Design by Kate Barraclough
Styling: Victoria Bell
Printed and bound by C&C Offset Printing Co., Ltd
10 9 8 7 6 5 4 3 2 1